Self-Defined

Edited by Sara Nelson
Designed by Tina Strasberg and Kayo Der Sarkissian

Published in 1999 by
Stewart, Tabori & Chang
A division of U.S. Media Holdings, Inc.
115 West 18th Street
New York, NY 10011

Distributed in Canada by
General Publishing Company Ltd
30 Lesmill Road
Don Mills, Ontario, Canada M3B 2T6

Library of Congress Cataloging-in-Publication Data

Self-defined
        p.   cm
    ISBN: 1-55670-937-4
    1.Self. 2. Self-perception. 3.Women—
    Psychology. I. Self
    BF697.S4334 1999   99-28694
    155.2—dc21   CIP

This book was printed and bound
by Toppan Printing Company, Ltd., China

10 9 8 7 6 5 4 3 2 1

First Printing

ACKNOWLEDGMENTS

This book is the brainchild of SELF magazine's Editor-in-Chief Rochelle Udell whose vision and generosity made its creation one of the happiest of publishing stories. But the story really began back in 1979, when S. I. Newhouse, Jr., Chairman of The Condé Nast Publications Inc., realized the need for a magazine that applauded the strength of women: SELF magazine. Not surprisingly, all of us who worked on this book have strong visions and strong voices; Art Director Tina Strasberg, Photo Editor Frannie Ruch, and I also had more fun than you're supposed to compiling the writings and art that appear here. Committed to the idea that "you can open it to any page," we worked to provide the clearest images, the cleverest jokes, and the pithiest pronouncements on *self*—but we couldn't have even partially succeeded were it not for the generous contributions of the writers and artists themselves, most of whom worked for a pittance so that we could fill the coffers of Girls Incorporated®. Thanks also to Kayo Der Sarkissian, who pulled us out of the fire at the last minute, and to the ever-patient SELF magazine staff and freelancers, particularly Judy Daniels, Emily Listfield, Kati Korpijaakko, Jane Praeger, Adam Glassman, Phyllis Levine, Meg D'Incecco, Diana Benbasset, Christine Brennan, Plaegian Alexander, and Molly Lyons. SELF's Publisher and Promotion Director, Beth Brenner and Cheryl Marker, were invaluable, as were Laura Morice, Carmela Ciuraru, Ruby Cutolo, Susan Mulcahy, Akira Yoshimura, and Bonnie Turner. Our compatriots at Girls Inc.—Alex Kopelman, Andrea Nemetz, and Anastasia Higgenbotham—were always ready and eager to help us bat around ideas and come up with plans. At Stewart, Tabori & Chang, we'd like to thank Leslie Stoker, Michelle Sidrane, Helene De Rade Campbell, and Deirdre Duggan for their faith and hard work. Rarely does one get the chance to work with such a diverse, intelligent, funny, and dedicated group of people, self-starters all. Thank you.

Sara Nelson, Editor
Self-Defined

ABOUT *SELF-DEFINED*

For 20 years, we at SELF magazine have been exploring all aspects and definitions of *self*—the physical, spiritual, emotional, psychological—and how they're integrated. In planning for our anniversary this October, we developed a list of favorite "self" words: self-employed, self-made, self-image, self-esteem, self-loathing, self-renewal . . . you get the idea. Then *we* got the idea to phone, fax, and E-mail this list to some of our favorite writers, artists, photographers, and celebrities—women, children, and men. "Which word resonates with you?" we asked. "Will you take a few words and/or images to define it?" In essence, we were asking these talented individuals—each of whom defines the very concept of *self*—to take a "self" word and give it meaning.

This is no easy assignment. *Self* is one tough word to define. It's individual and collective. It's Eastern and Western. It's the foundation of you and a reflection of your culture. Self exists alone and in relationship to others. It changes as you change, morphing through every age, upheaval, and triumph in life. Self is why you can simultaneously feel like one in a million and one of the crowd. It fills the space within you and around you, and connects and disconnects you with everything in your life.

Some of our contributors came at their "self" words head-on. Others backed in, and a few dared to hang off the cliff to find meaning. Everyone took this assignment very personally. You'll probably laugh at some of their contributions. We hope so. Others might make you cry. (Ditto.) All prove that a healthy self—not to mention a lot of self-knowledge—is the key to happiness, success, love, and well-being.

Building healthy "selfs" is the business of SELF magazine. Girls Incorporated® is in the very same business. This nonprofit organization inspires girls to be strong, smart and bold, and to confront the subtle societal messages about their value and potential. This is important work. To ensure that it continues, a percentage of the profits from the sale of this book will go to Girls Incorporated.

So, please, sit back, read. And enjoy yourself.

Rochelle Udell, Editor-in-Chief
March 1999

"IF I AM
NOT MYSELF,
WHO WILL I BE?
AND IF I AM
ONLY FOR MYSELF,
WHAT AM I?"

—THE TALMUD

Introduction: The Meaning of Self

by Shirley Abbott

"There is that in me—I do not know what it is—but I know it is in me."
—WALT WHITMAN, "SONG OF MYSELF"

"Self" was a word first spoken thousands of years ago by people whose names and ways remain a mystery. In Indo-European, the mother language from which hundreds of modern languages descend, the original syllable denoting "self" may have been something like "s(w)e," according to modern linguists. From this root, dozens of words were crafted and handed down in dozens of languages, for example, not only "self" but also "secede," "seduce," "secure," "solitary," and "suicide." The swift separation of the one separating from the many is palpable in all these words.

In English "self" is noun, pronoun, adjective. It morphs restlessly from one gender to the other (himself, herself) and then to neuter (oneself, itself). If you look at any dictionary, under "self," or at the titles of the pieces in this book, you will see how this word, which you might think denotes introspection and exclusion, combines obsessively with other words and fragments, like a particle of oxygen seeking a bond. In French and other Romance languages, where "self" is related to the Latin word *sui,* self is expressed as "same"—the *moi-même* of French, for example, or *soi-même* (oneself) or as those tiny vocables—*me, te, se*—that appear before a verb and turn its action back toward the self, or subject.

The grammar of "self" surely grows out of biology. An infant's first intellectual task is to distinguish between itself and the world. This need to make a distinction is embedded in our basic chemistry. The immune system is on red alert for "nonself" and will mount an attack when it detects the smallest bit of nonself (*aka* foreign) matter.

Americans have no corner on "self," but in order to function, a democracy requires each of us to assert the right to a self. Our Constitution begins, "We the people...," but that other document on which our politics is founded entitles us to the pursuit of happiness, a footrace we must undertake singly, one by one.

A century and a half ago in *Leaves of Grass*, Walt Whitman spoke eloquently about the beauty of self, especially in his famous "Song of Myself" from that volume. The public was shocked. What right had a shaggy free-verse poet to "celebrate and sing" himself? One critic called Whitman a pig rooting in garbage. The poet's employer thought the book offended "the rules of decorum and propriety," and our first great singer of self lost his job.

"Self" can, of course, be wholly self-ish. But what is called the self yearns to combine with other selves, to blend with the "form complete," as Whitman called the universal self. He knew this could be a perilous quest. Yet, only by creating a self, and many selves within that self, can we connect with others. It is a lovely paradox that creating oneself is the first step toward love.

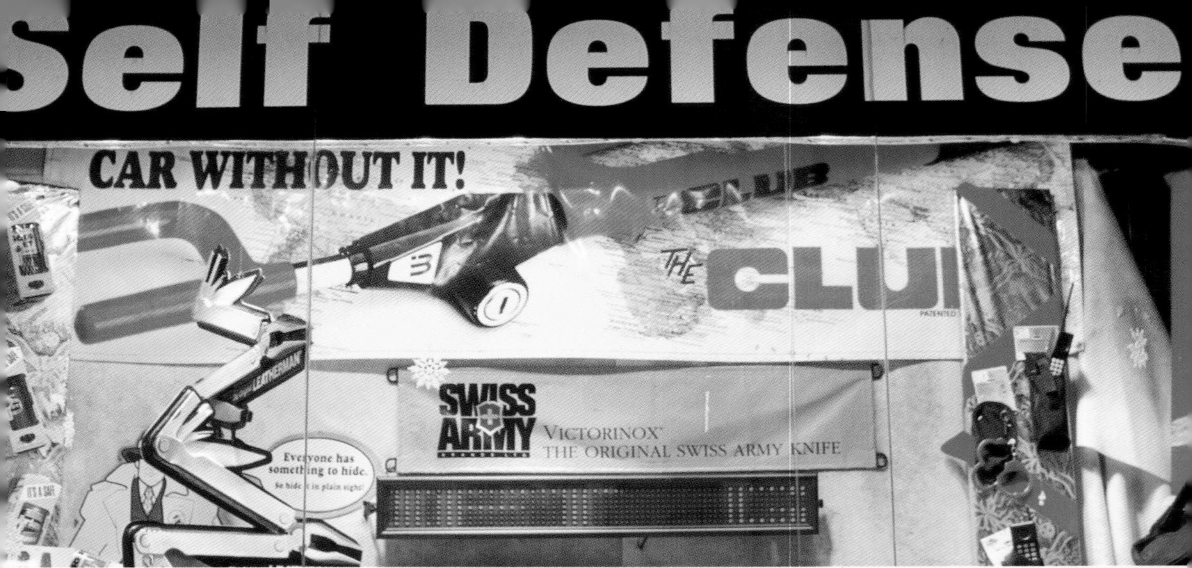
Self Defense
CAR WITHOUT IT!
THE CLUB
LEATHERMAN
SWISS ARMY
VICTORINOX
THE ORIGINAL SWISS ARMY KNIFE
Everyone has something to hide.
So hide it in plain sight!

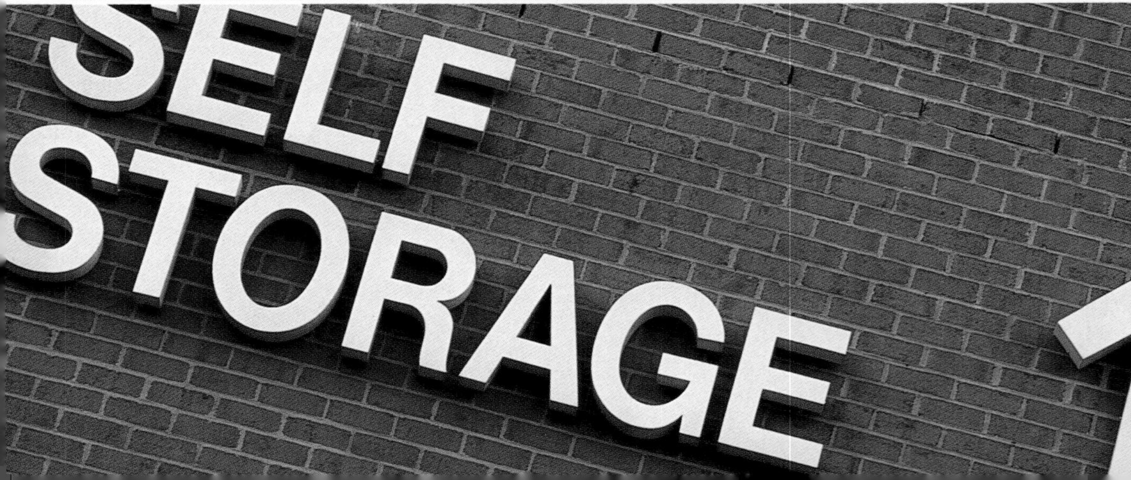
SELF
STORAGE

TOP LEFT: GEOFFREY CROFT; BOTTOM LEFT: MARK FINKENSTAEDT; RIGHT, CLOCKWISE FROM TOP: GEOFFREY CROFT,

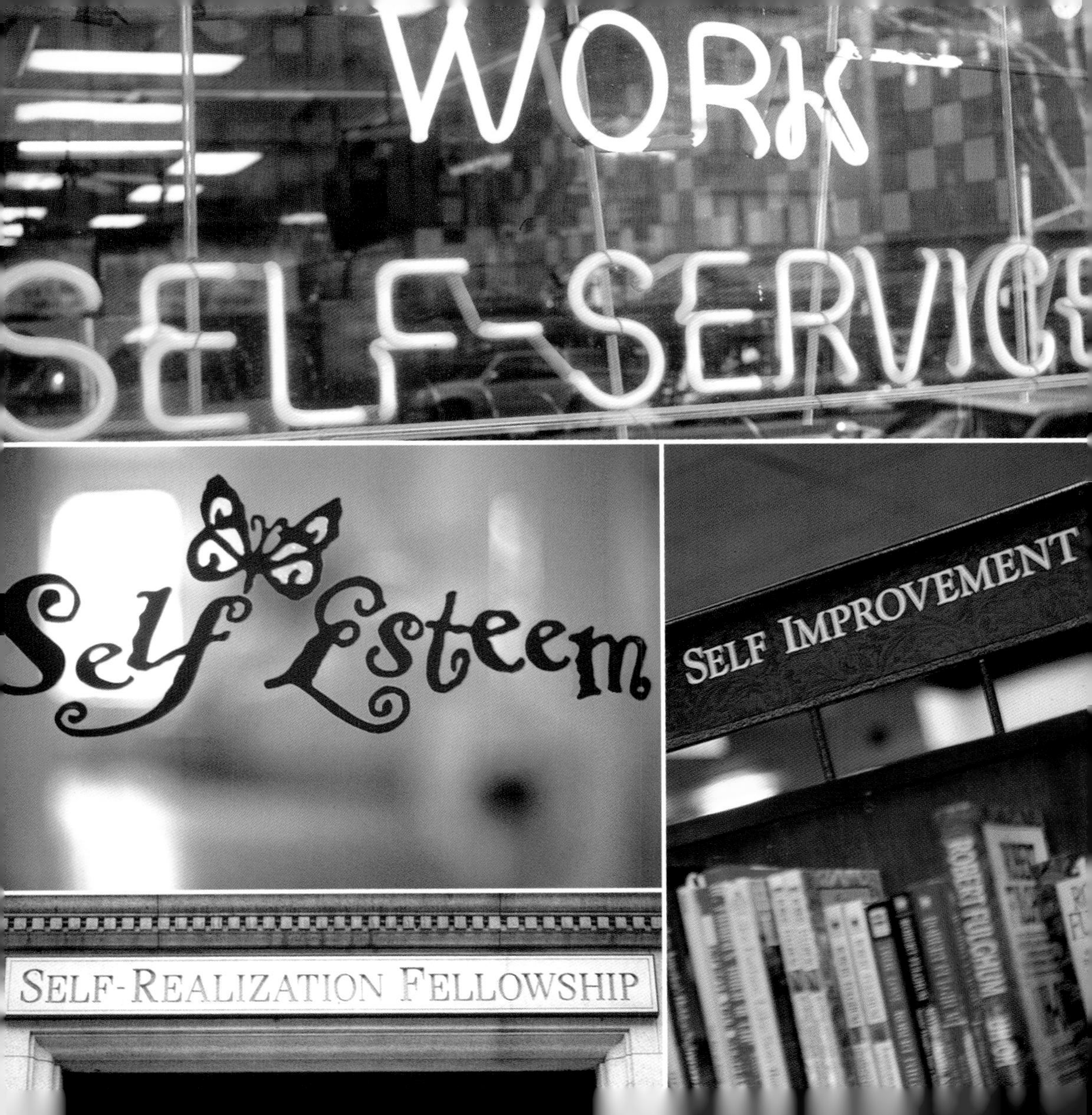
WORK
SELF-SERVICE
Self Esteem
SELF IMPROVEMENT
ROBERT FULGHUM
SELF-REALIZATION FELLOWSHIP

✪ Self-Absorbed

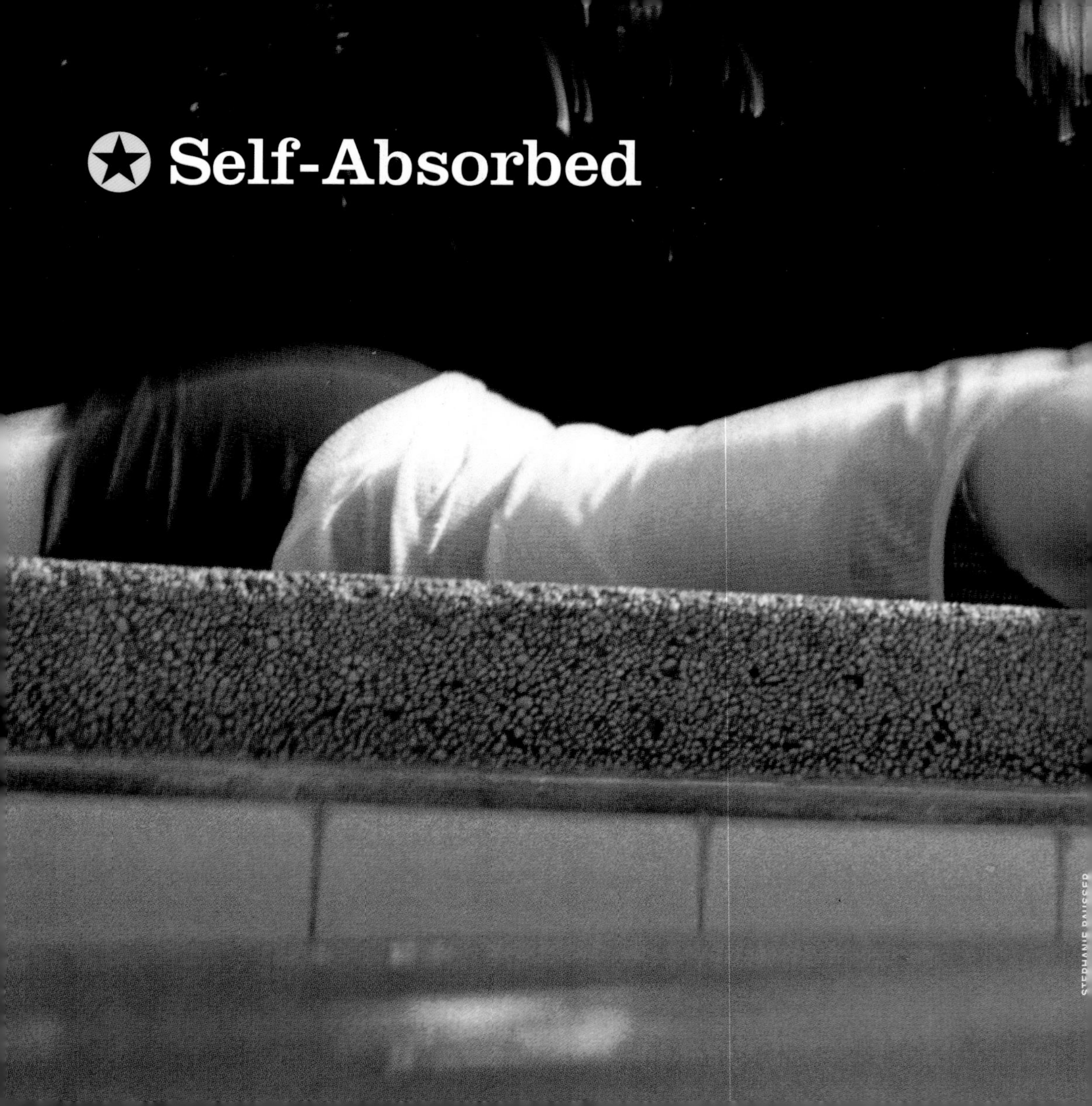

STEPHANIE RAUSSER

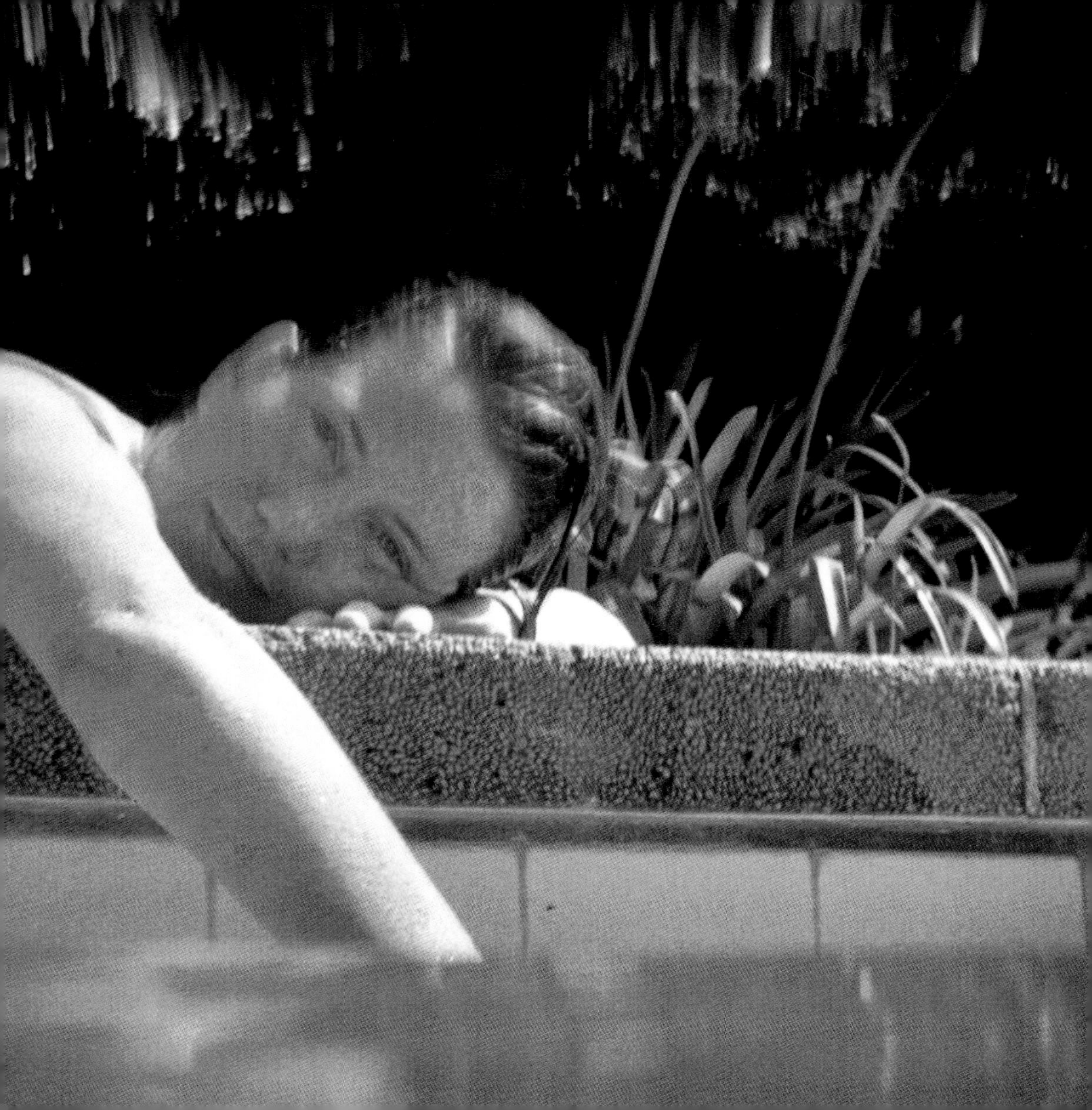

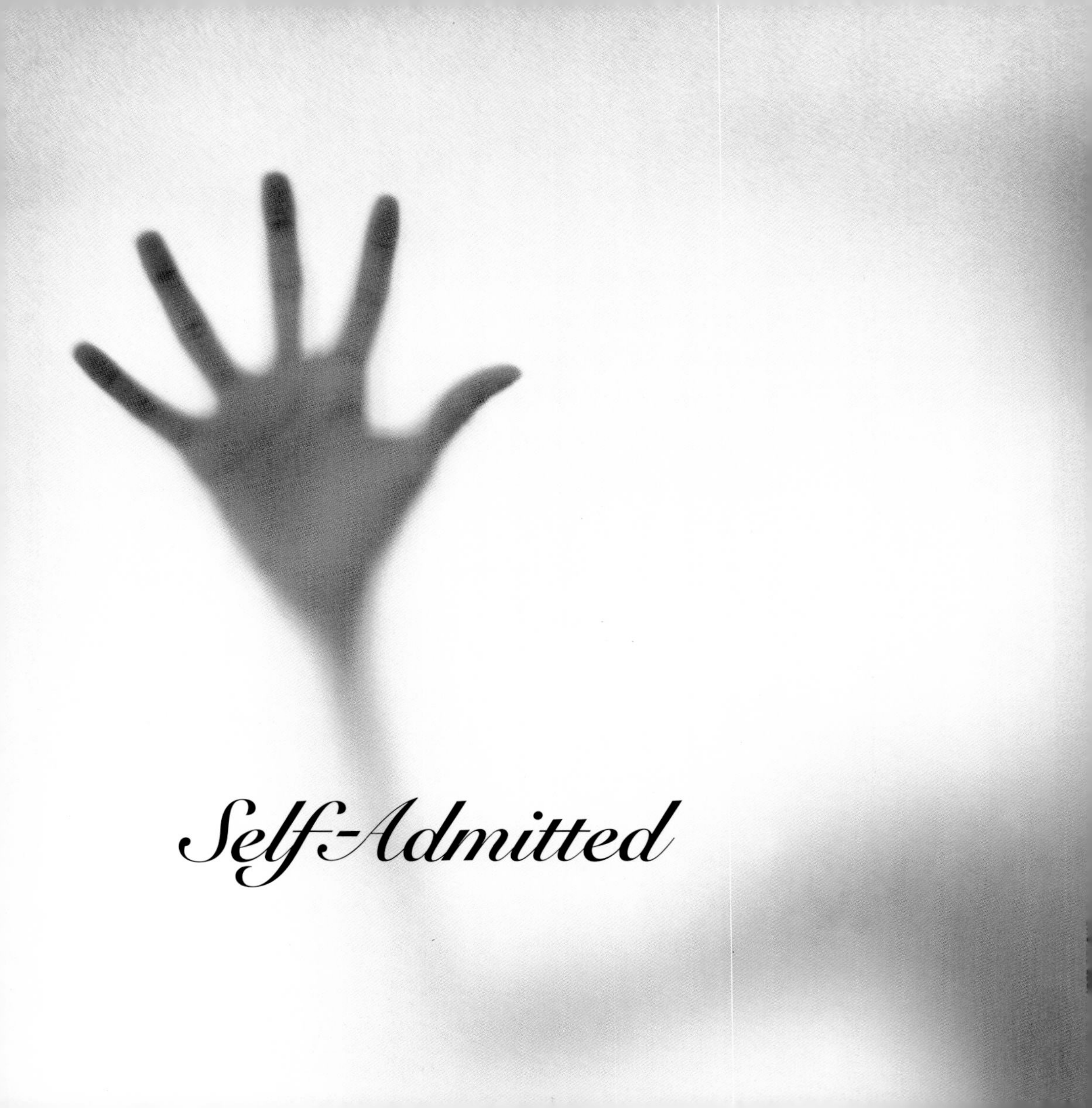

Self-Admitted

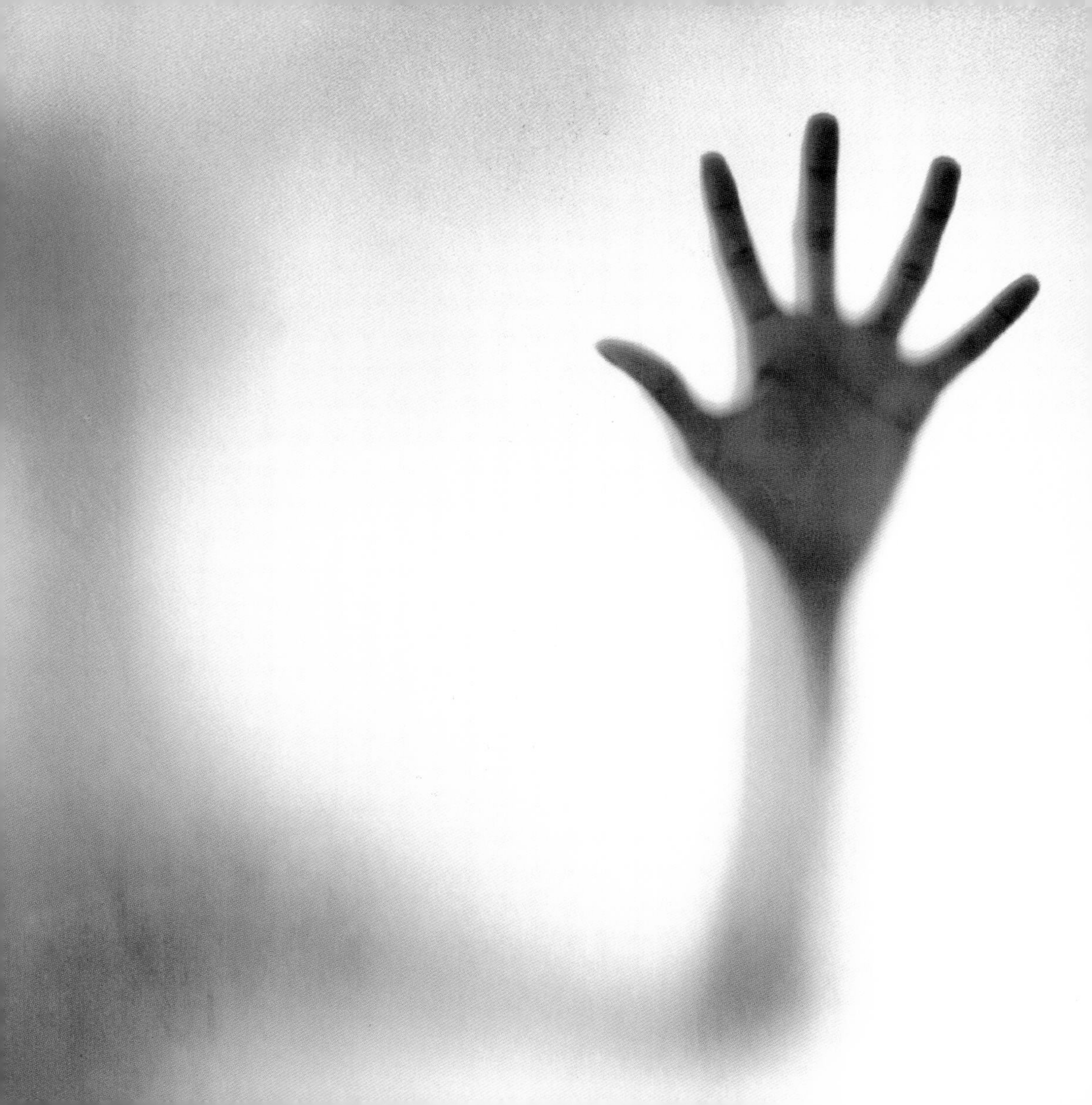

SELF-ADVERTISEMENT

STEPHANIE DOLGOFF
New York, New York

OBJECTIVE

To land a mid-maintenance man for a romantic relationship with security, room for advancement, and good benefits. Man must have legal means of financial support and at least a vague idea of the location of key parts of the female anatomy. All other points negotiable. Am willing to relocate.

EXPERIENCE

CARETAKER OF BOYFRIEND JOSHUA DEYO
April 1991 through April 1992
- Invented specialized techniques (patent pending) to remove day-old pizza from venetian blinds and creatively camouflage cigar burns in linoleum.
- Sharpened olfactory sense to the acuity level of a special agent in the K-9 unit in order to detect source and location of offending odors—without having to move furniture.
- Cooked—and memorized—the entire table of contents of *The Art of Jewish Cooking.*

GIRLFRIEND TO JIM O'BRIEN
September 1990 through January 1991
- Implemented all functions necessary to the operation of an unsigned rock-and-roll band, including hauling heavy amps, fending off groupies, critiquing "experimental" new sounds, and removing dive-bar smells from clothing.
- Responsibilities included crisis mediation between feuding band members and one-on-one counseling sessions assuring boyfriend he's not as worthless as his father thinks.
- Organized fund-raisers to keep musician/boyfriend in beer and cigarettes between gigs.
- Promoted from one-night-stand status after six months.

MANAGER OF JEREMY MICHAELS
October 1987 through June 1989
- Handled the fragile ego of a fledgling actor, commenting favorably and convincingly on every unremarkable walk-on (as well as voice-over) actor/boyfriend had during full course of relationship.
- Created catchy, self-esteem—boosting slogans such as "You're not getting a gut; it's all muscle."
- In the role of image consultant, reversed years of style influences by convincing boyfriend to let a professional cut his hair and that galoshes, while useful, are rarely necessary.

SPECIAL SKILLS AND INTERESTS

Fluent in Brewski, Sportspeak, and other languages that employ grunts and gestures.

SELF-AGGRANDIZEMENT

CHUCK SHOTWELL

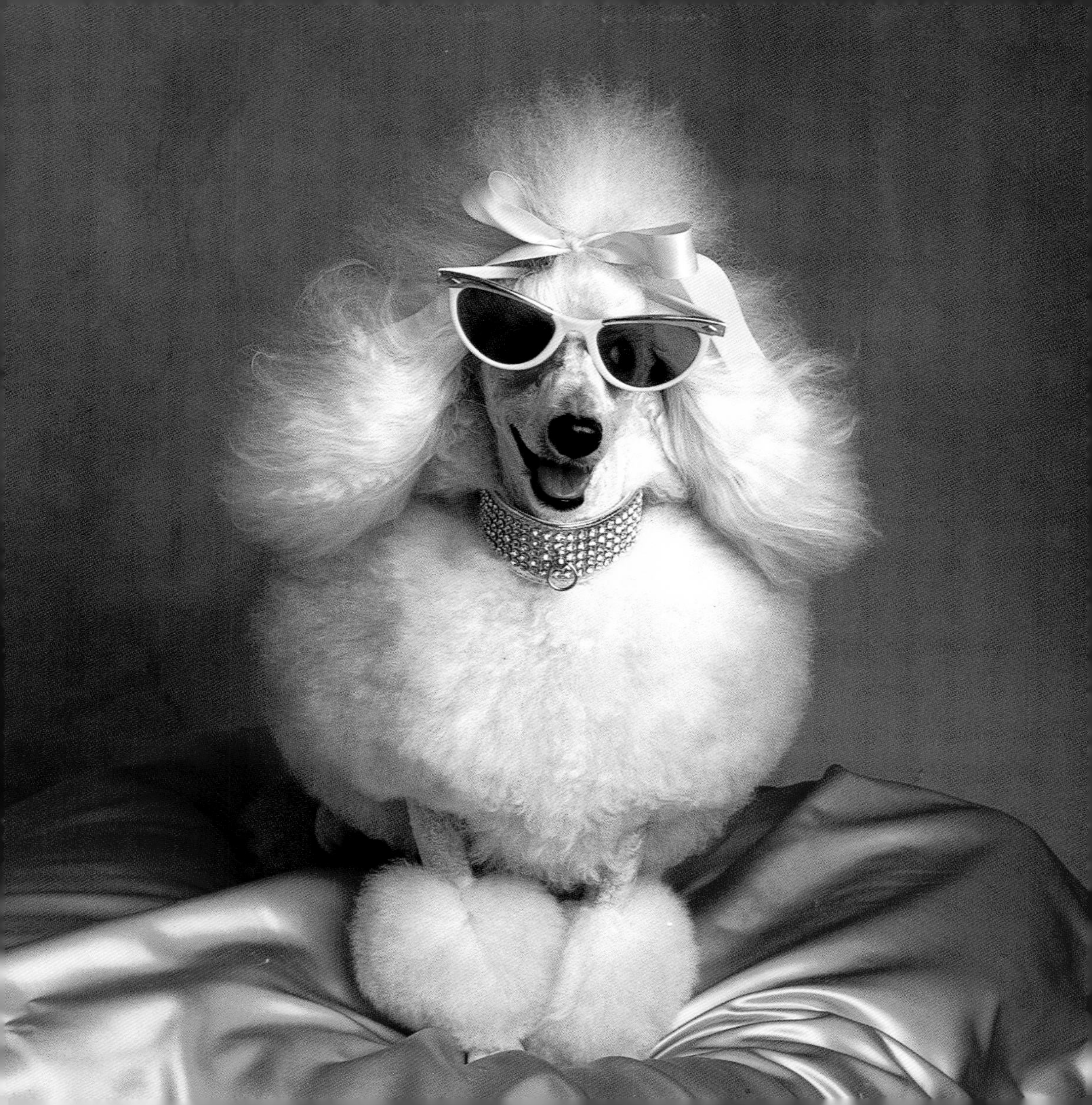

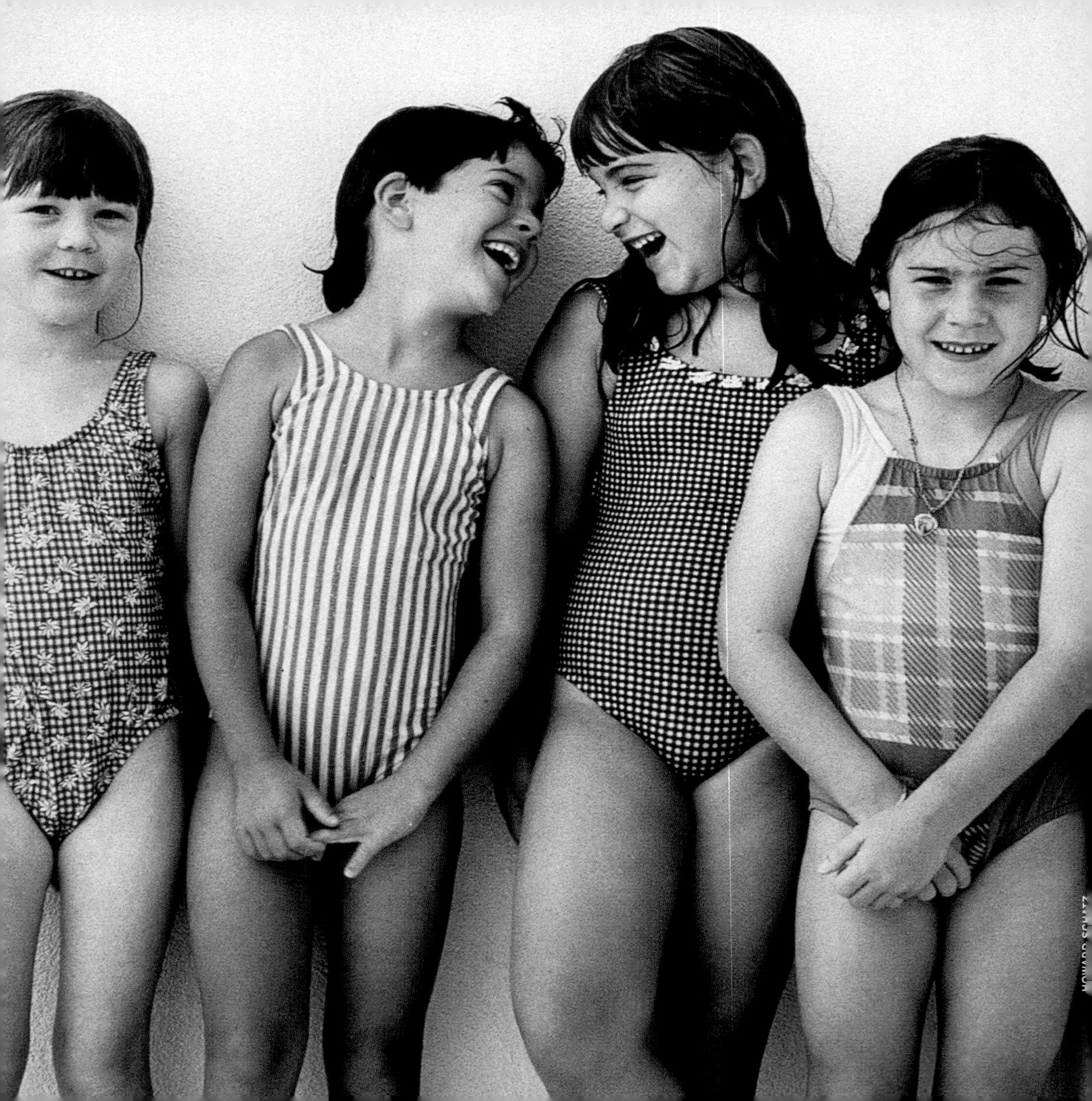
HOWARD SCHATZ

Self-Amused

SELF-ASSURANCE

BY RUTH WHITNEY

The best thing about self-assurance is that it is contagious.
One self-assured person can calm a small riot, unite a crowd,
inspire a team, turn a jury around.

And self-assurance grows with age. When a woman is described as
"a self-assured 20-year-old," chances are what is meant is that for a
20-year-old, she is self-assured.

When a woman is described as "a self-assured 40-year-old" you can be sure
she is decidedly self-assured. There is a kind of gravitas that self-assurance
gains with years.

Self-assurance says, "I belong here."
Self-assurance says, "I deserve it."
Self-assurance says, "I will win."
But self-assurance also says, "Take your turn."
Self-assurance says, "I can wait."
Self-assurance says, "I can share."

Self-assurance knows how to compromise—and why, and when.
Self-confidence can be brash and cocky.
Self-assurance is calm and centered.
Self-confidence can be chipped away at.
Self-assurance is rock solid.

So who has self-assurance?
Hillary Clinton comes to mind. She keeps her cool in the eye of a raging hurricane.
So does Martina Navratilova, a champion who followed the rules and made some of her own.
And Katie Couric, who holds her ground, smiling her sweet smile all the while.
And Connie Morella, the Republican representative who distinguished herself by voting *against* impeachment.
And Anna Quindlen, who skipped out on her huge success at *The New York Times* to follow her writing star and to be a mom to her kids.
And Jodie Foster, a daring actor and director who even had her baby her way.
And Madeleine Albright, who handles affairs of state and personal business with equal amounts of wisdom and honesty.

These are all famous women. But take a look around you.
Who in your life has self-assurance?
In mine, it would be a high school Latin teacher. And my sister.

One more thing: It's not easy to fake self-assurance, but it *can* be done.
And nobody does it better than William Jefferson Clinton.

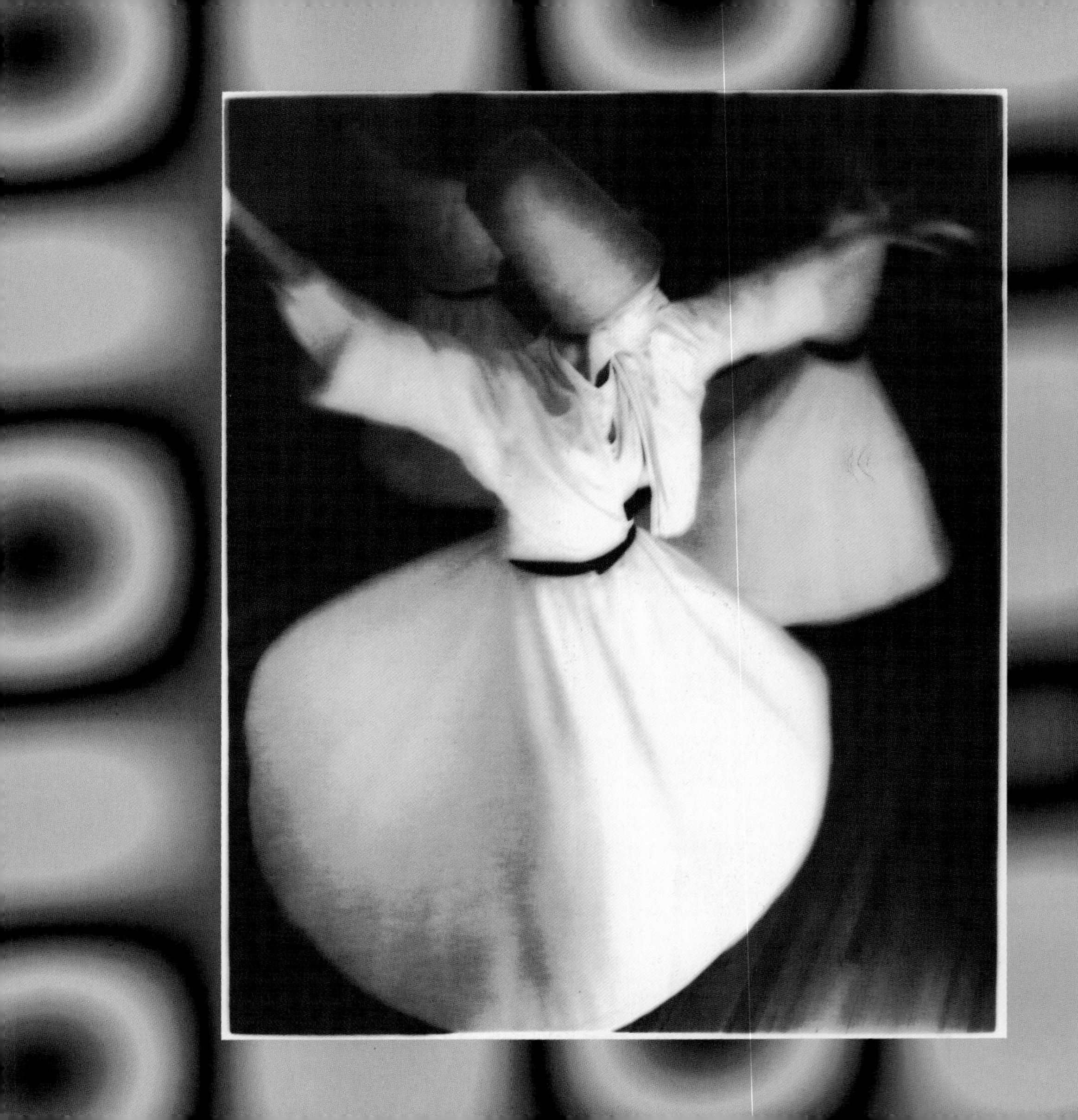

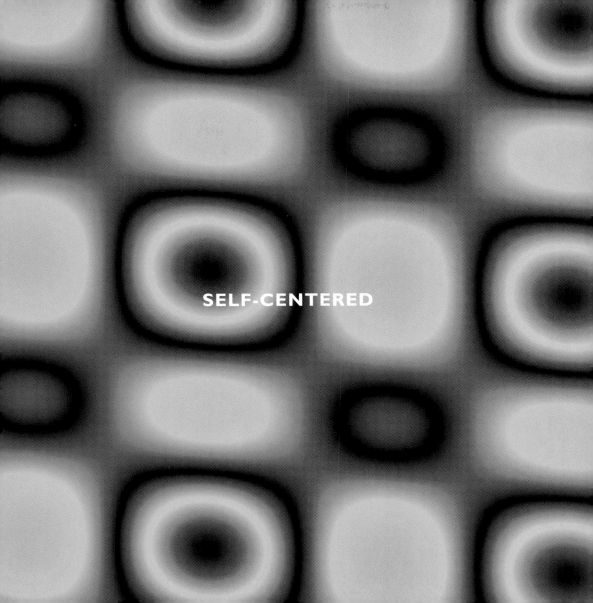

SELF-CENTERED

self-cleaning

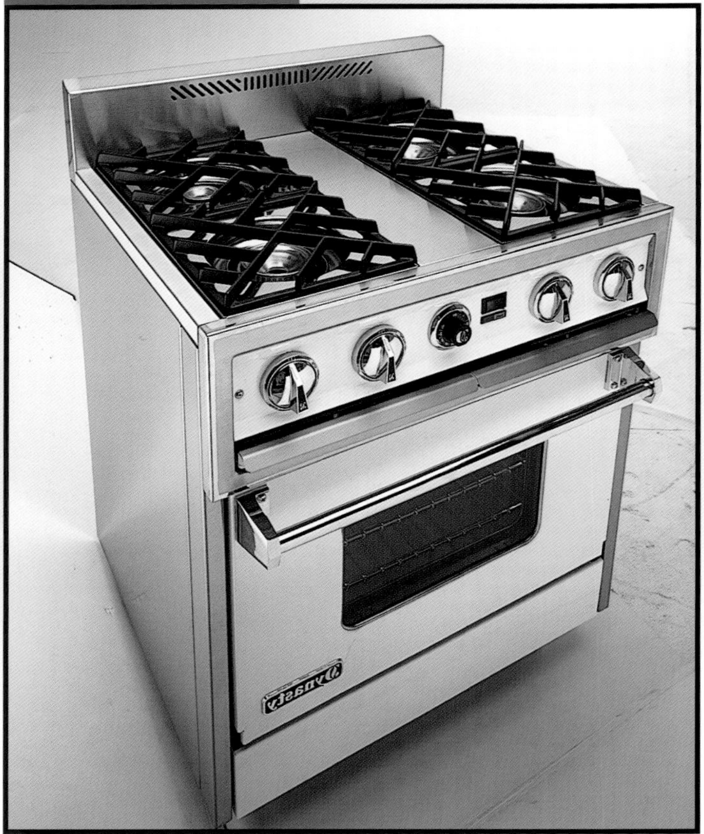

LEFT TO RIGHT: DAVIES + STARR; PETER GRIDLEY/FPG; COURTESY OF MOVADO

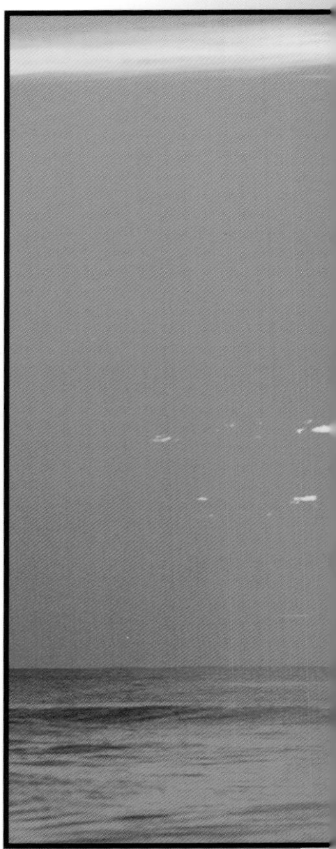

self-operating

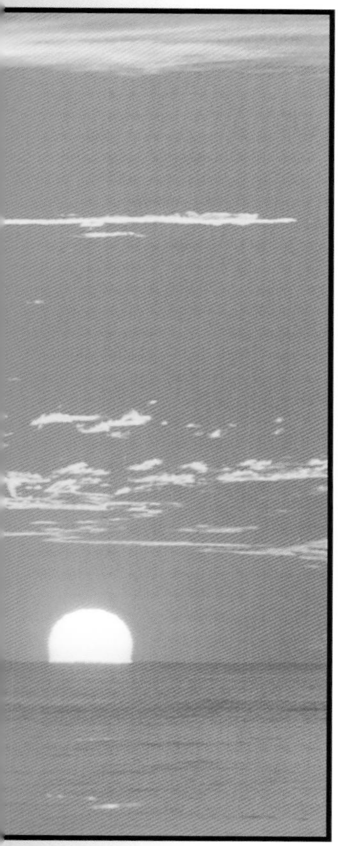

self-winding

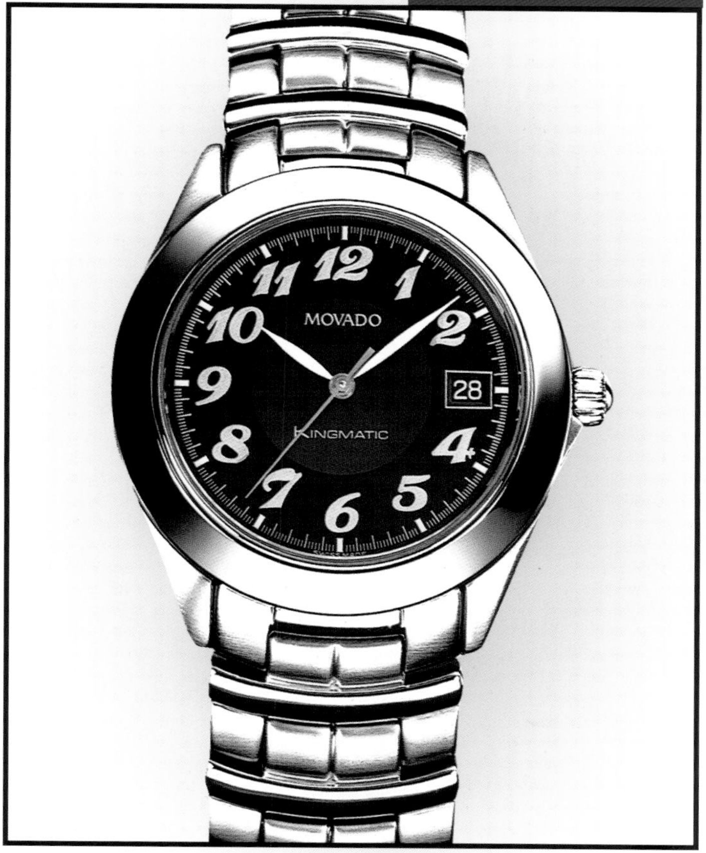
MOVADO
KINGMATIC
28

"Be yourself
more than you
thought of

and you'll be ever being."—Janis Joplin

SELF-CONFIDENCE

by Liza Nelson

Self-confidence is one of those qualities, like beauty and brains, that I've always wanted for myself but have always distrusted in others exhibiting more than a slender allotment. By others, of course, I mean other women. Self-confidence implies a certain brashness, a certain swagger. Self-confident men are attractive men. Self-confident women are, well, they're intimidating—at least to women like me who, when praised for a job well done, assume the world has them mixed up with someone else.

I'm not talking about self-esteem here, that amorphous sense of being a person of intrinsic worth. I have plenty of self-esteem. So do the majority of women I know, even those of us most neurotically lacking in self-confidence. But unlike self-esteem, self-confidence is determined in the concrete realm of specific activity. Can I get the job done, and done well? That's the question behind self-confidence.

There are skills so completely beyond my capacity, like anything to do with music or biology, for which self-confidence is irrelevant. Does a cat worry because it can't behave like a dog? There are tasks such as cooking and mother-hood that I love, and they come so naturally to me that issues of confidence never surface. And then there are all the other skills, tasks, and challenges I care about but might or might not be able to accomplish. With those, my circular logic takes over: The more succeeding matters, the less sure I become of my ability; the more success becomes uncertain, the more succeeding matters.

If confidence requires a certain aggressiveness, a certain willingness to put oneself forward in the world, lack of confidence got me off the hook for years. I have spent my adult life writing—articles, poems, stories—all the while loudly doubting my ability to write. It was soothing being told I wrote better than I thought I did by friends whose judgment I could discount because they liked me. I read every rejection—and there were plenty—as the Godlike voice of authority and discounted every whisper of praise out of fear that once my hopes were raised, they'd be flattened that much more dramatically. But now my first novel has been accepted for publication and now strangers will see it. I'm petrified, but not as petrified as I thought I'd be.

Yeats once said "Confidence comes from repetition, from the breath of many mouths." I'm not sure what changed my relationship with self-confidence— whether it was being told enough times by others that I could do it or sitting at my desk day after day until I proved that I could. Probably a little of both— but either way, I have to face the even more frightening thought that I've become a more confident person.

Talk about intimidating.

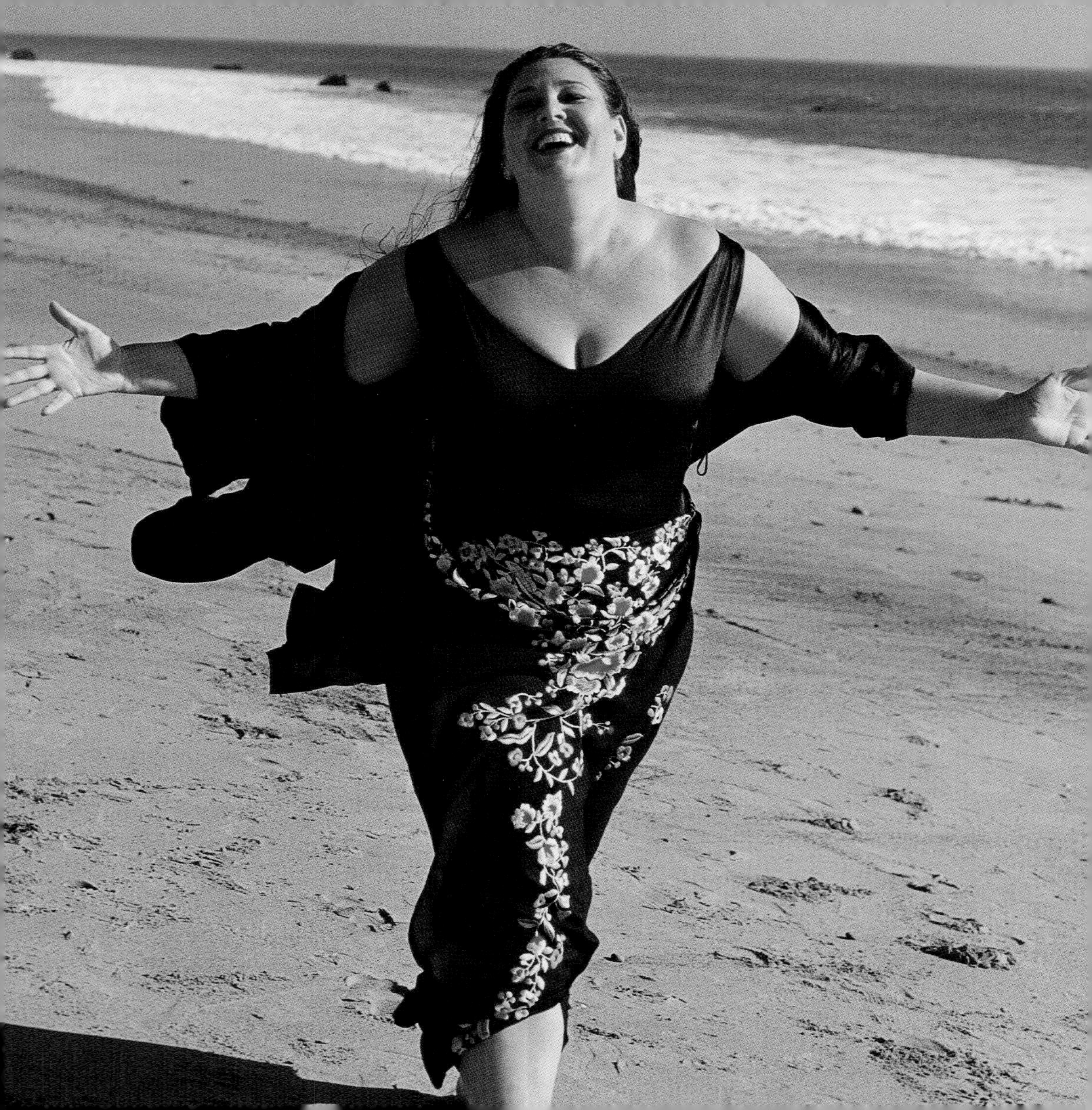

Self-Confidence

"You have to be brave or pretend to be brave. The person with the most confidence wins."

–Camryn Manheim

Self-Confidence

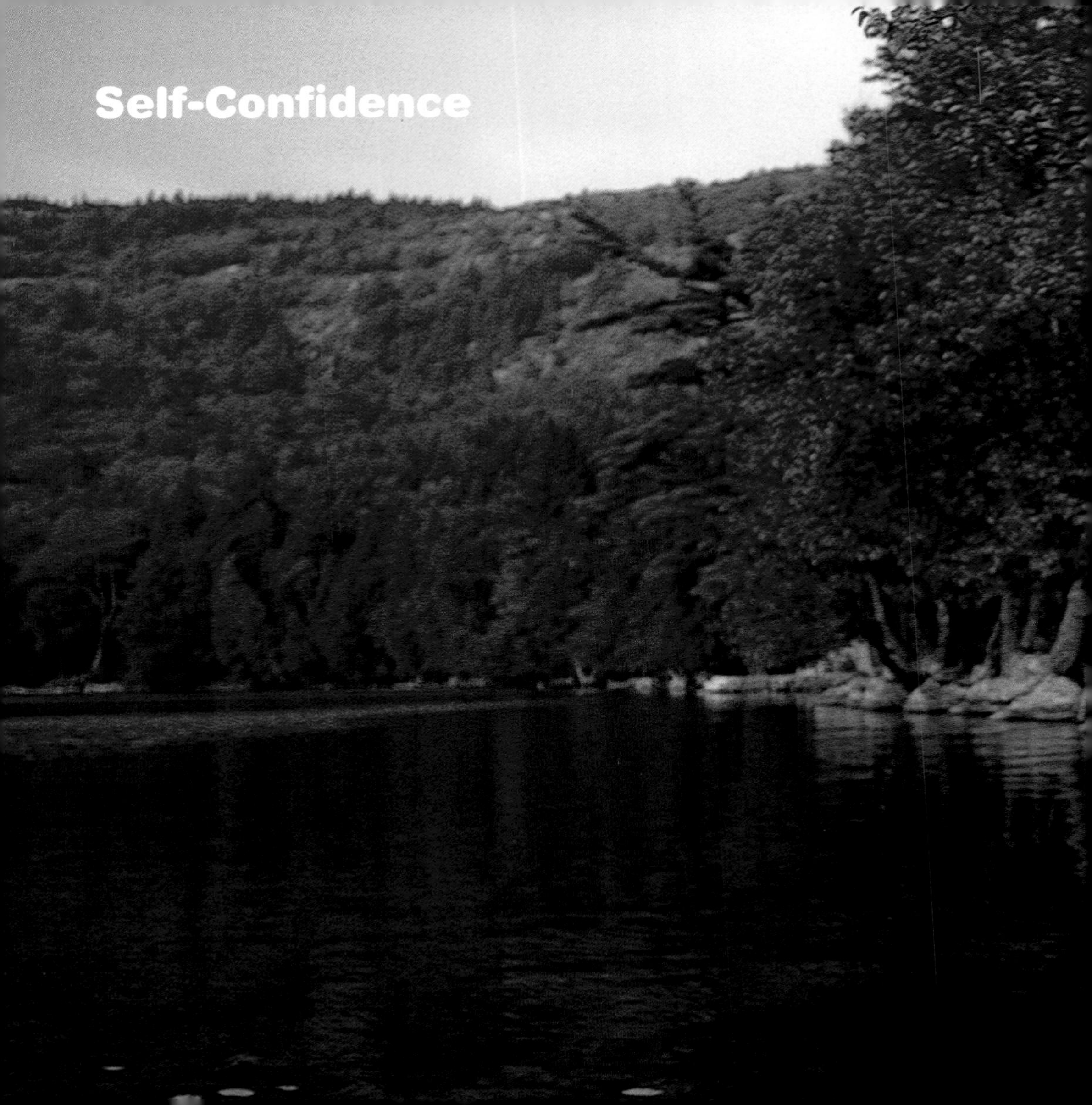

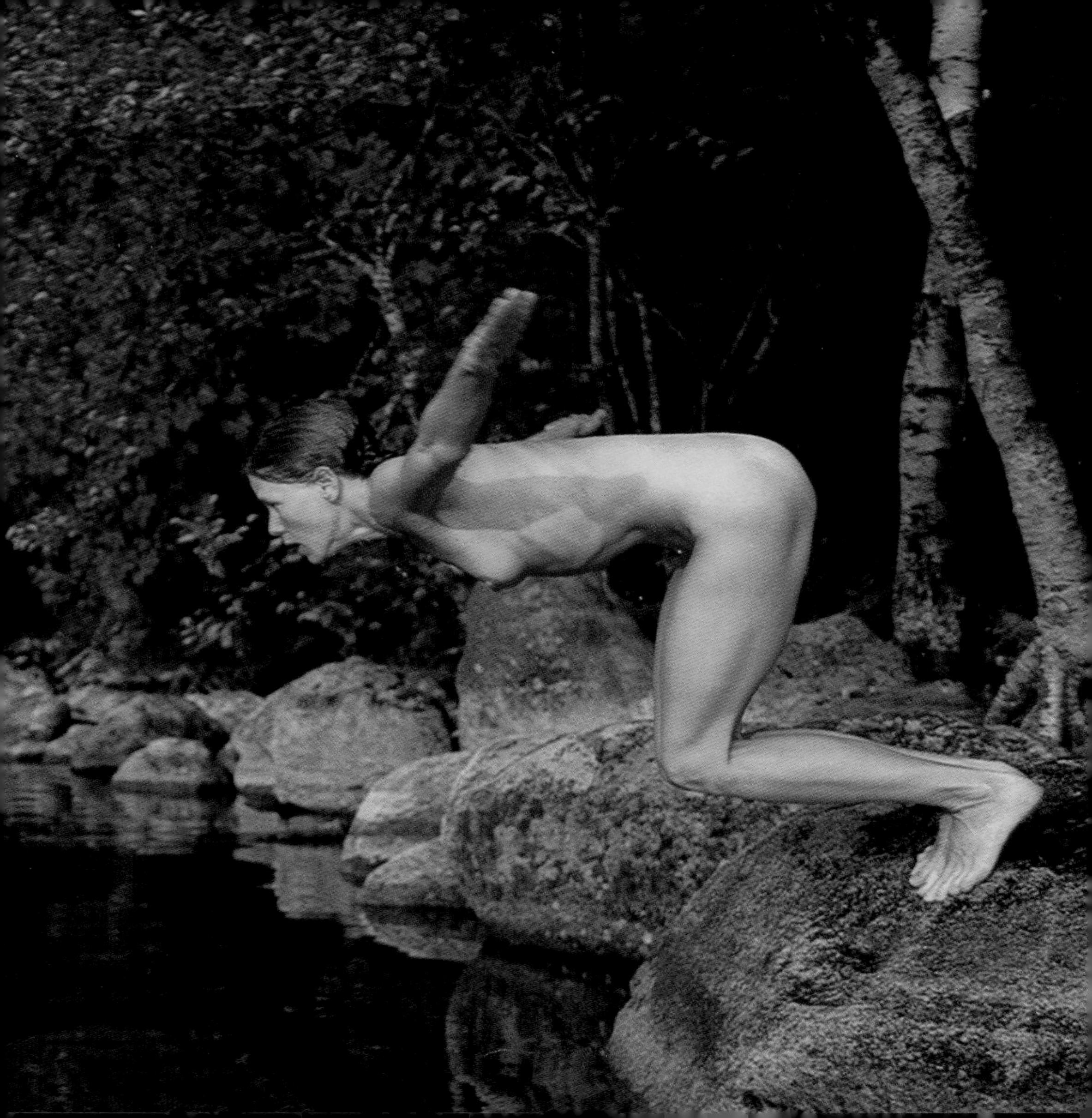

SELF-CONS

by Alain de Botton

It was one of the first character traits she mentioned. It had started in childhood—perhaps because her teeth were asymmetrical and she had to wear glasses, or because her parents were divorced and there was no money, or because she looked more like a boy and loved math. In any case, for as long as she could remember, she had watched herself as though she had been someone else, and it had hurt.

With age, Helen had tried to put the self-consciousness behind her. She had constructed an ironic, playful exterior. "Wouldn't you rather be talking to someone more interesting in the main room?" she had said the first time we met, in the kitchen at the birthday party of a friend, where she was playing with the hot wax that was rolling off a candle like tears in slow motion. "I hate big parties; I'm silly enough that they make me self-conscious." And she smiled a flash of the asymmetrical teeth.

In the early hours, lovers may be tempted to play a dangerous game. With their heads resting on the same pillow, one may whisper to the other, "Why do you find me attractive?"

A woman may not believe her lover finds it adorable that she worries about the mole on her chin, that she hates her glasses and thinks others must mock, that she can't quite pronounce her s's properly and is embarrassed when talking to sales assistants in shops because, as a hangover from childhood, she imagines they will think her unable to pay for what she has chosen.

He couldn't love my self-consciousness, she thinks, until she recalls that the object of a relationship is intimacy, and that the catalyst of intimacy is vulnerability. "It is by revealing all I cannot share with others that I cement my particular allegiance to you." Because self-consciousness is a sign of vulnerability and therefore a promise of intimacy, those who suffer from it are often enchanting. The gappy teeth, moles, scars, strange mispronunciations, and glasses are routes to a more private person; they are the indispensable gateways to the soul.

Self-consciousness is routinely condemned because it suggests a preoccupation with oneself. Yet, those devoid of self-consciousness invariably prove offensive. From self-consciousness, there often flows sensitivity to others. It is because we worry what others will think of us that we grow attuned to their needs and chip away at our flaws.

To ensure that we are interesting, it is vital to worry we may be boring. To be loveable, it helps to wonder whether we are not hateful and uninteresting—and to float the thought that perhaps an attentive stranger should prefer to talk to someone else in the other room.

Self-Contained

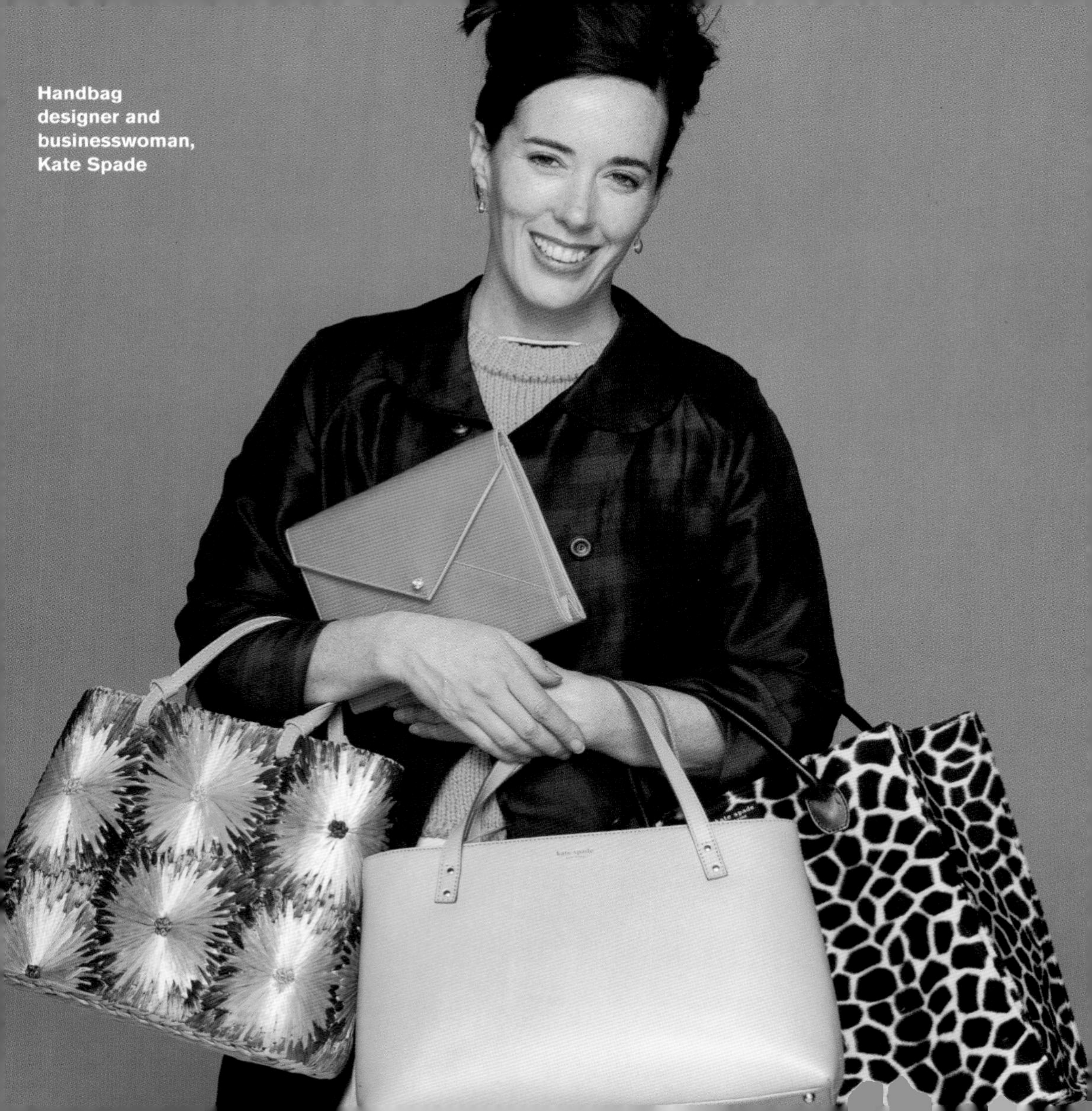

Handbag
designer and
businesswoman,
Kate Spade

Self-Contained

by Bebe Moore Campbell

One Saturday when I was about 12, I couldn't find a friend to accompany me to a movie I wanted to see. "Go by yourself," my grandmother commanded. I did. And I walked home alone, too, taking narrow backstreets where I found myself reflecting on the story I'd just seen, mimicking the characters' accents and mouthing their lines. That day I realized that I could have fun all by myself.

It was a valuable lesson, one that I've had to learn again and again. Like everyone else, I've sometimes equated being alone with being unchosen. But each time I embrace solitude—whether by reading a book, taking myself out to lunch or writing—I've learned that I can choose myself.

And when I do, I discover something powerful about myself: the ability to love and validate my own ideas and my life in a way no one else can. Alone is the place where I find the courage to do that.

My goddaughter came to me not long ago, brooding because some of her high school friends were mistreating her, yet she desperately wanted to be a part of their group. I bought one ticket to a play I thought she'd like, and on the night of the performance I dropped her off at the theater. When I picked her up two hours later, she was standing on the sidewalk, a little apart from the theater crowd. She got into the car without saying a word. All the way home there was a dreamy look in her eyes. I hope she discovered that night what I learned years ago: The most important lessons in life aren't learned in a crowd, but by being in tune with the stillness of one's own heart.

SELF-CRITICAL

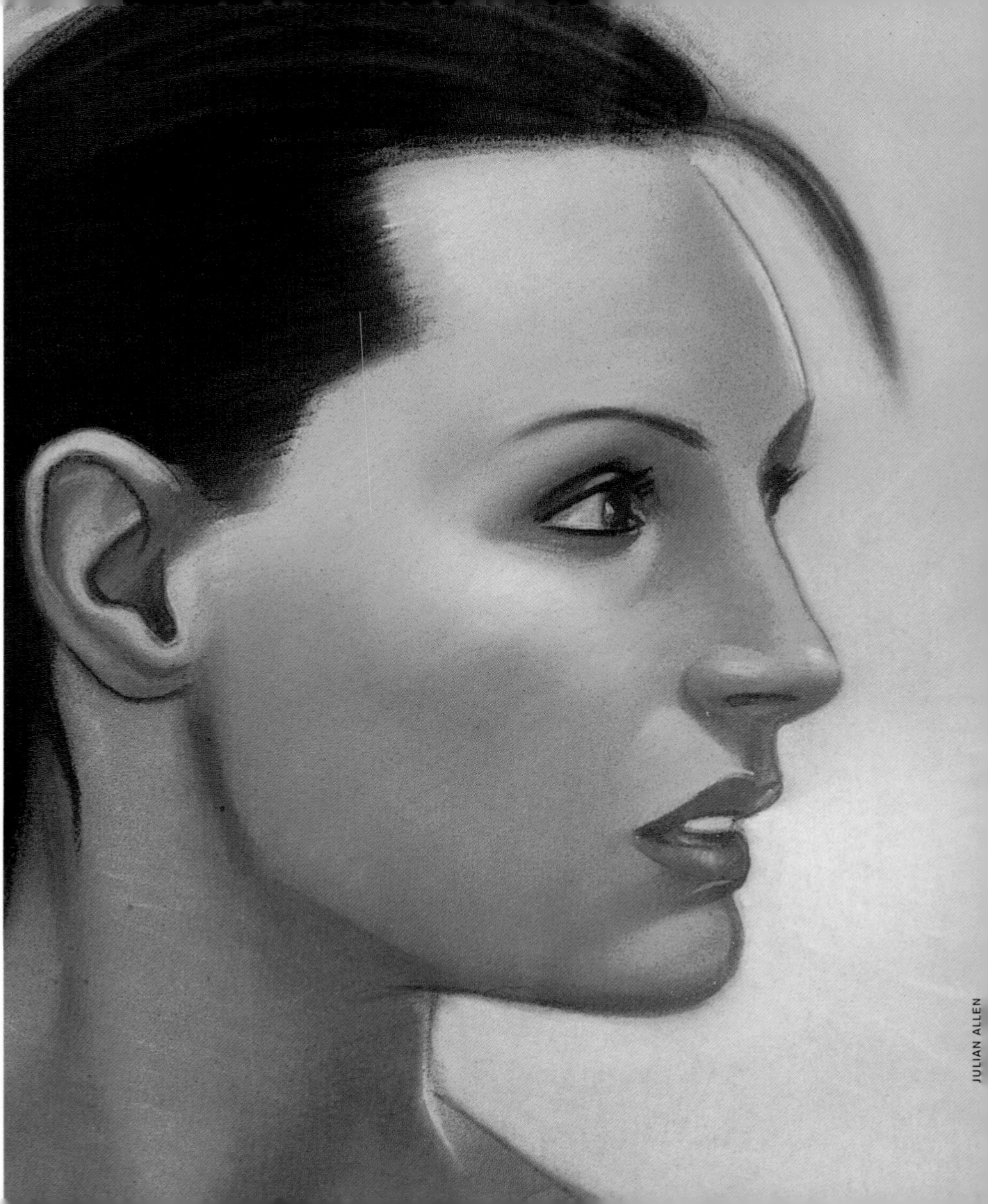

JULIAN ALLEN

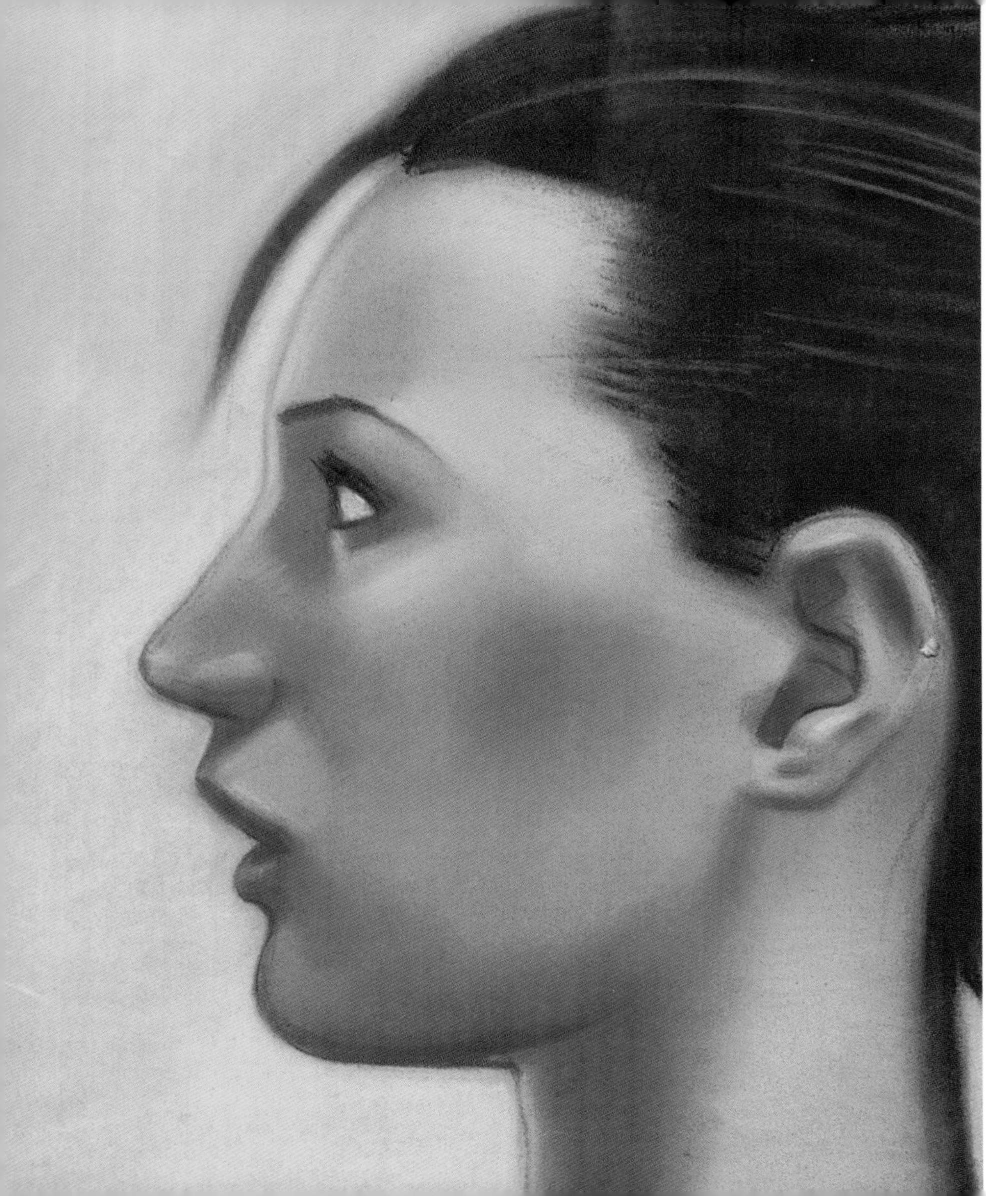

SELF-CRITICAL

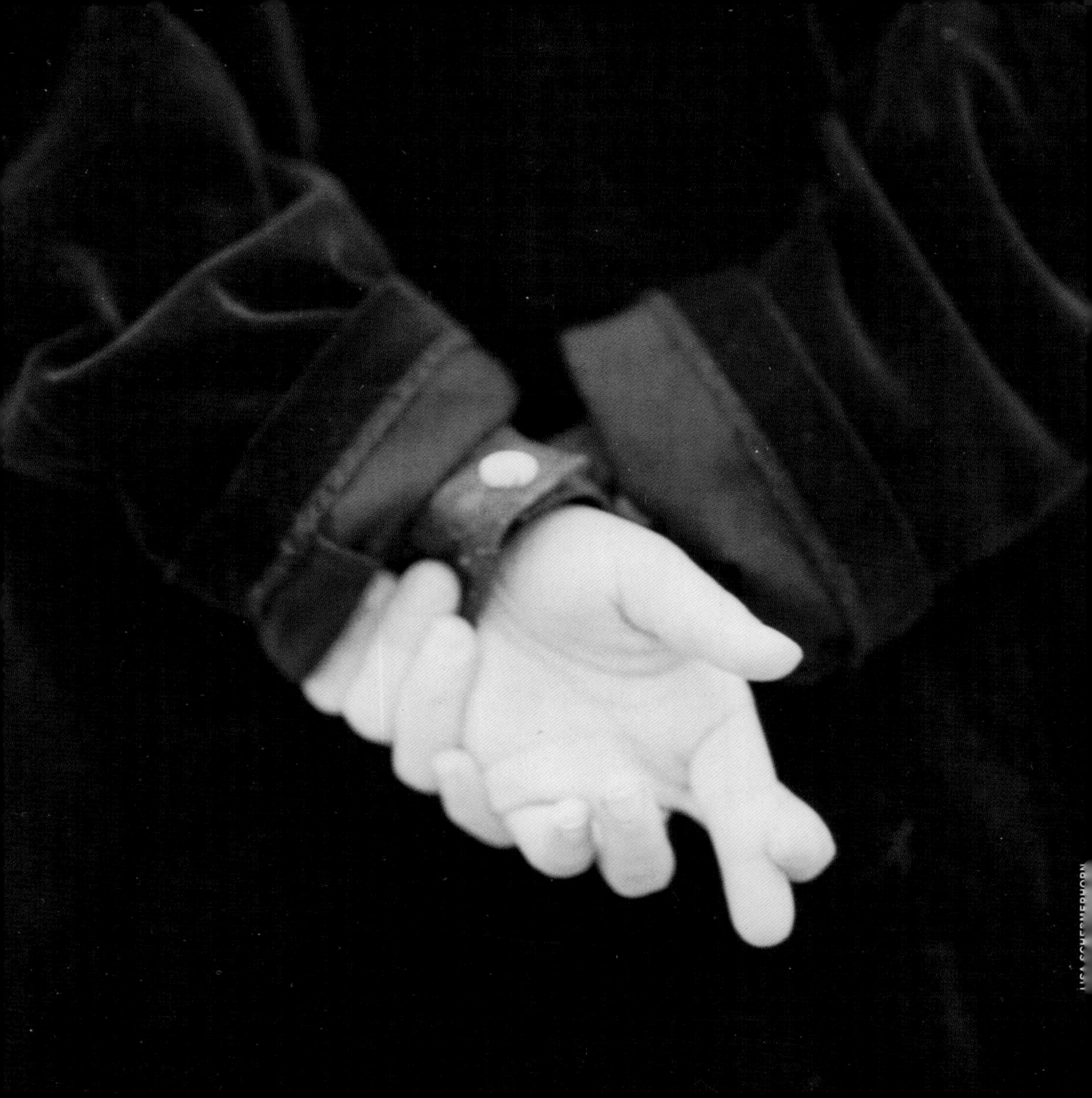

Self-Deception

"To lead astray or frustrate oneself,
usually by underhandedness."

MERRIAM-WEBSTER'S COLLEGIATE DICTIONARY, TENTH EDITION

SELF-D

BY LINDA FAIRSTEIN

When I graduated from law school in 1972, there was not a prosecutor's office or police department in this country that had women and men trained to deal with the issues of sexual assault, domestic violence, or child abuse. Our laws were so archaic that they prevented victims of rape from testifying in a courtroom unless there were independent witnesses who could prove the legal elements of the case—a very rare occurrence and a completely absurd requirement.

The New York County District Attorney's Office, the best in the country, had only a handful of women on its legal staff, and none of them was allowed to prosecute murder cases. The work, Mr. District Attorney himself told me, was too grim and tawdry for women like me.

Clearly, I thrived on tawdriness—because I followed my passion for this long-neglected cause. Then, as now, I believed in self-defense for women—self-defense on the personal, political, and public fronts.

As it turned out, so did a lot of other people, most of them not the lawyers and judges who witnessed cases involving traumatized women every day in their courthouses.

Rather, it was those in the groundswell of the women's movement who adopted a well-known male sports metaphor as our battle cry: The best defense is a strong offense. We "took back the night," as we called it in the seventies. We learned to view women who had been attacked as survivors, not victims. We hurried to change the laws, and with greater difficulty, the attitudes that had for so long prevented us from having our day in court.

FFENSE

What we've accomplished is simply astounding. Consider:

- A rape survivor no longer needs corroboration for her court case.
- She cannot be cross-examined about her sexual history.
- Stalking has been recognized as a serious criminal act, and has been outlawed everywhere.
- We have learned that the greatest time of risk in a relationship is when a woman chooses to separate from her partner—and that society must provide her with meaningful options to ensure her safety.
- Every community, large and small, is developing support services to aid women in crisis.
- DNA technology relieves a rape survivor of the sole responsibility for identifying her attacker.

Pretty impressive for 20 years—but even these pale in comparison to the real accomplishment. That is, the awakening of the public consciousness; more and more women come to me and my colleagues today and place their trust in our hands, knowing that they can, at last, triumph in the courtroom and achieve justice in these cases. That is what has kept me at this work for more than a quarter of a century.

I beg to differ with you, Mr. District Attorney. Our jobs may have been, at times, somewhat tawdry, but to me, they have never been grim. Two decades of teaching self-defense to women: I'd call that challenging, exciting, and uplifting.

Self-Def-

by Karen Elizabeth Gordon

As much as I revel in being one of the boys and taking my pleasures as a woman, it is my girlhood that I treasure with an unflagging affection for the word *girl* itself, through shifting fashions and prescribed preferences. *Gal* gets my hackles up and *chick*, in the days when it was bandied about, I could just about take—but in referring to me, only when preceded by *foxy*. *Broad* is asking for trouble, although its intensive use should have coincided with the shoulder-pads era. Years of exposure to the BBC have left me with a fondness for *lass*, but that's not likely to catch on here, while *woman* reaches the height of its sonority in low-down lyrics: It sounds best to me in the blues. I would take umbrage on any woman's behalf at her being addressed as "old girl," a humiliation I have thus far been spared. *Baby* as a term of endearment, is endearing only through a French or Yugoslav accent. I dissolve in mirth, knowing my friends learned it from American movies and songs and that these guys are exploiting the self-conscious strangeness and continental charm that they bring to their mimicry. *Girlie* has amused me ever since I put the word in the open mouth of a cocky little dragon, who used it in the fetching come on: "Hey, girlie, drag your carcass over here!"

As for *girl*, while it offers beauty to the eye and ear, it also contains a growl *(grrrrl!)*. It rhymes with many a precious object and motion: pearl, ə-'nish-ən

curl, whirl, unfurl. It is tenderness and promise, the essence that stays with us through the process of becoming; it is impetuosity, flirtation with no end in mind—an outlaw in a skirt. In my fictions, even cowboys get their girlhoods with tawdry trappings and turns of phrase. William Spackman lovingly encircles this swirl of sound in the mellifluous title of his novel *An Armful of Warm Girl.*

Girl is of great expedient value in my conversations with myself, saving me long harangues on many aspects of behavior, and keeping the tone mock-serious: "Good girl" delivers its pat on the head, "bad girl" administers its spanking, while "naughty girl!" means I've been having fun—or am congratulating a friend on some fait accompli mischief. When we women use the word *girl*, it often feels collegial or conspiratorial. "Hey girl!" clangs with fellowship; "Listen here, girls" packs a frolicsome wallop of esprit de corps.

Ten years ago I abducted my Macedonian friend Epifany from Sacramento and a tragic marriage for a day's saunter through Berkeley's cafés, bakeries, and cheese shops, one after another irresistible, as fragrances pulled her through doorways, and flavors surrendered their secrets. I found myself caught up in her intoxication as her stirred senses sent her back into the years she had spent in Paris studying couture and learning the song "Notre Dame de Paris, Donnez-moi un Bon Mari." Old-world in many ways (always on hand to exorcise my bedroom of the visitants from bad dreams, or to tuck a piece of cake under my pillow on St. Theodore's Eve), Fany captured her excitement and wonder in this eloquent pronouncement: "Today, we are girls again!"

SELF-DELUDED

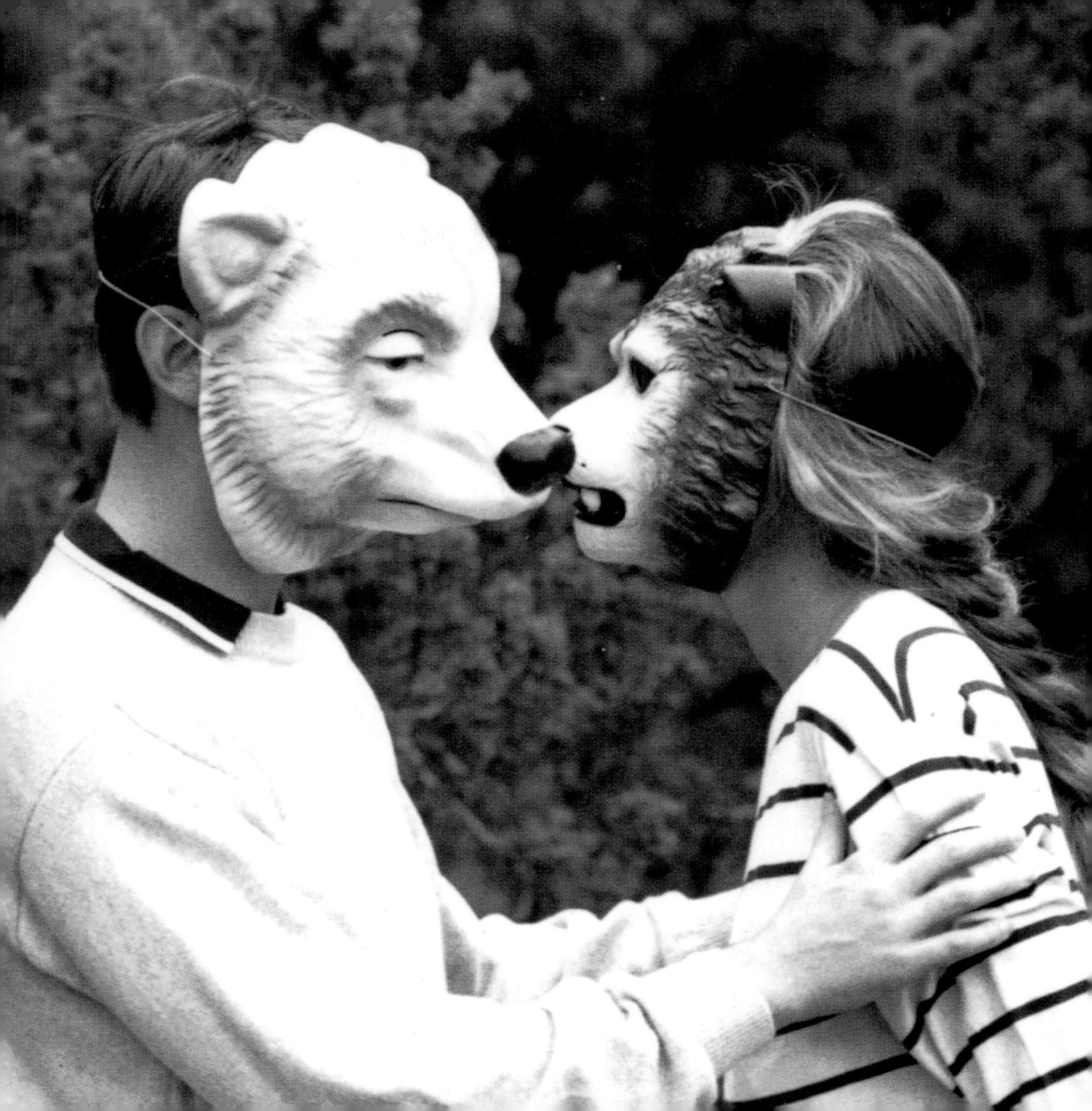

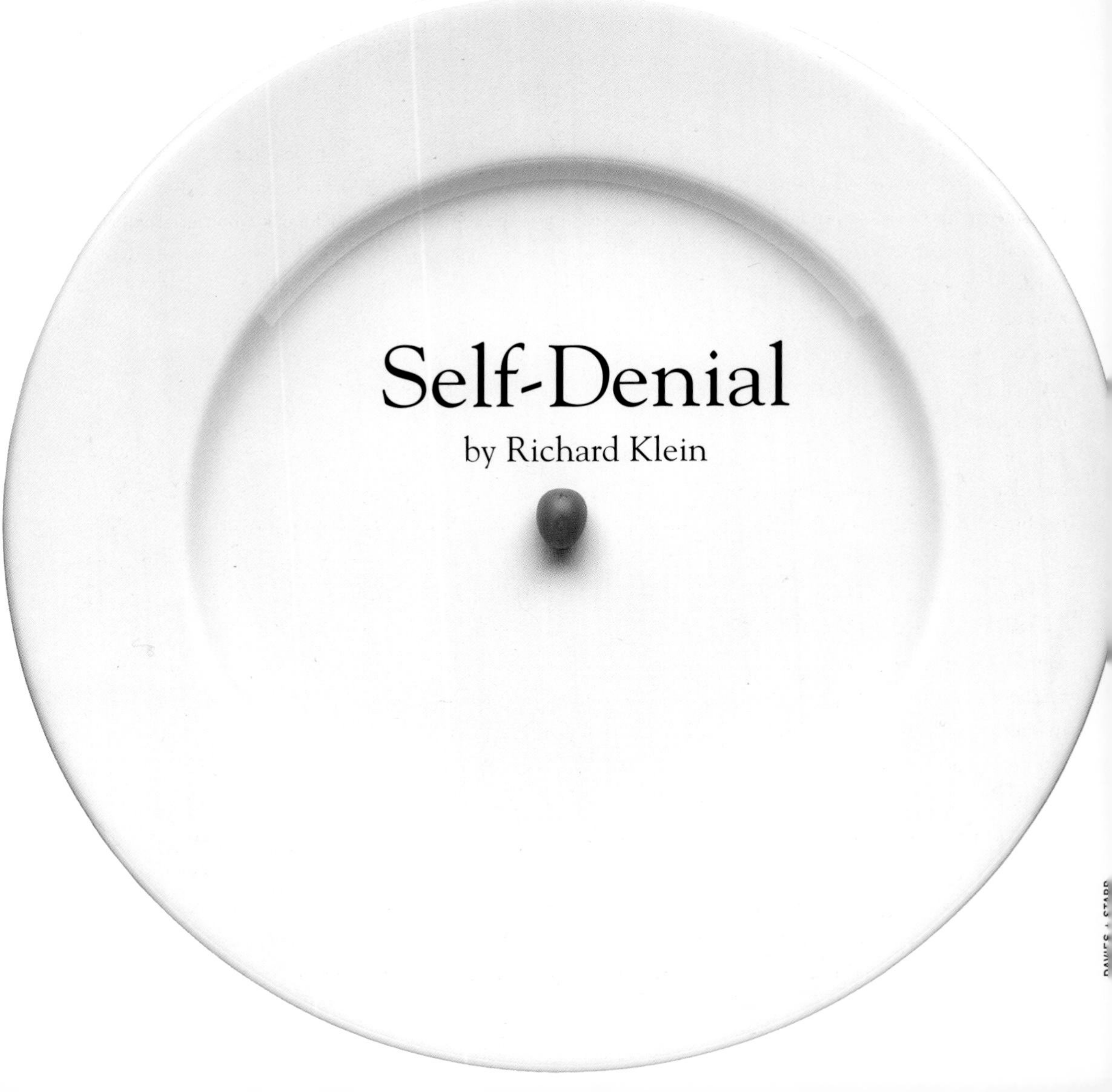

Self-Denial

by Richard Klein

DAVIES + STARR

Self-denial is a lot of fun. Take monks. You think they don't have fun? Maybe you suppose they give up every pleasure in this world—even talking—just for the sake of pleasure in the next. It's never that simple or calculated. Sometimes they get intense pleasure, not to say a lot of satisfaction, from refusing to enjoy opportunities for sex, say, that often are ready at hand. There's a kind of thrill in saying "No!" to whatever it is you might desire most in the world, when it offers itself to you for the taking. The further fact that it might be forbidden makes it naturally even more desirable. But the biggest high may come from holding a lit cigarette two inches away from your nose, rolling it slowly between your fingers and then stubbing it out! Or (excuse the example) have you ever had to go real bad and waited until it got seriously bad, just for the fun of it, for the shiver that comes when you just barely succeed in overpowering the urge? A lot of good sex is about self-denial, at least about the postponement of orgasmic satisfaction. It is a certifiable fact that if men don't take the time to postpone intercourse, women will likely enjoy it less. There's a lot of fun in holding back, denying yourself some pleasure in the interest of pleasure. When a long, elegantly shaped nail scratches your back with a ferocity just this side of cruelty, with enough pain that it almost starts to hurt, you know you can make it stop when you want to. But you don't. You deny yourself the word that would make the pain stop. Why? Not because you're deranged, but because you like the invigorating tension and the cruel lucidity you acquire in the harshest moments of self-denial when relief seems boring.

Self-denial is probably indispensable for art. Maybe van Gogh needed to deny himself his ear to paint *Starry Night*. But there's more to it. Take those spas that have sprung up widely. Sure, people go there for the results. But when you've been once and you think of going back, you discover that what you liked most about the time there was the pleasure of self-denial. Most of the time I can't deny myself a damn thing. If it's soft and white and in the refrigerator, I say "Yes!" But at the spa there comes a moment when instead of taking a little bit more food on your plate you decide to take a little less. It must be equivalent to the rush you feel at the gym when you push yourself to the burn, to the point of pain that comes from denying yourself the rest your muscles are screaming for. It's a physical rush but also a kind of moral triumph of the self over the self—over your body. Plato said the soul is a horse and rider. So self-denial is, thus, self-mastery, like taming and riding the horse you are.

SELF-DEPRECATION
by Susan Isaacs

Self-deprecation at its loveliest is **Noël Coward** referring to his comic genius as "a talent to amuse." It is a response that acknowledges and, at the same time, minimizes a gift, thus making the gap between you and less-blessed mortals not quite so vexatious.

Most of us tend to be somewhat less graceful.

An example of how self-deprecation more often manifests itself: A woman to whom you've just been introduced has sunlight-catching, silky-textured tresses. Indisputably world-class hair. Okay, now, whatever else is going on twixt you and her—an income tax audit, a discussion of Being or Nothingness—she spends the entire time in your company either twirling said hair about her finger or resourcefully flipping it up so, as it falls, it cascades over her shoulders like a scarf of moonbeams. Inevitably, you find yourself saying something like: "Hey, you've got great hair." She might, of course, answer, "Thank you." But then she'd risk being found guilty of the great American social heresy—a display of overt pride, which suggests she might not believe that we are all created equal. Thus, more often than not, she'll reply, "It's so limp on humid days like this." It is a response that lacks not only wit, but truth. You wind up not merely loathing her hair, but loathing her.

We Americans are usually less urbane than Coward, less skilled at self-deprecation. Like the hair lady, some of us whistle and stomp to call attention to our gifts. We want to make damn sure we get the chance to devalue what is ours. Too many of us take self-deprecation even further. Instead of using it as a means of touting our own good qualities to our fellow citizens, we use it as boom box to broadcast our bad ones. We children of immigrants are still, it seems, a little nervous about tyrants and bullies; we degrade ourselves before the bad guys can—in hope of stirring up enough pity or condescension to get them to lay off.

David Letterman goes on (and on) about the dreadfulness of his TV show. Howard Stern does likewise about his minuscule penis. Read an interview with any supermodel and you'll get the fungible don't-hate-me-because-I'm-beautiful quote: "I was so skinny and awkward in high school I never had a single date." In a culture that reveres public confession of weakness, it's very easy to confuse self-deprecation with self-loathing. If only we could all be more like Coward who, among his many other talents, realized that the only truly valuable "Hey, look!" always comes from the observer, never from the observed.

In the beginning, I climbed mountains as a hobby, clinging to the sides of glaciated peaks for, I always believed, the sheer challenge of it. I pursued summits to know that I had the physical and mental fortitude to go *mano a mano* with the imposing and unpredictable power of nature and come out on top. Part of the challenge, I suppose, was the risk of death, but I had never really felt its frigid breath on my neck. I was certainly unprepared when cancer was thrown into my life—and almost took it.

I almost died in an isolation cubicle while undergoing chemotherapy; then I underwent a bone marrow transplant. By the time I left the hospital two months later, I had experienced the ultimate challenge: facing death and embracing it as part of life. To combat the fast-growing cancer that

Self-Deter

had spread through my body, and the debilitating treatment that followed, I had to summon an inner strength I had not needed before—a strength I was not certain I possessed.

Climbing mountains has since taken on new significance—not as isolated moments in time when I challenge myself physically and mentally, but as part of a larger picture in which I challenge myself to experience life without compro-mise. In coming close to death, I realized the value of life; I overcame my fear of dying. One doesn't con-quer cancer—although it's possible to survive it for a long time—but what one does survive is the fear of death. So a life without com-promise is, for me, one in which I strive daily to follow my instincts and dreams wherever they take me. To quote a favorite saying of mine, "The point is to add life to your years, not years to your life."

mination

by Laura Evans

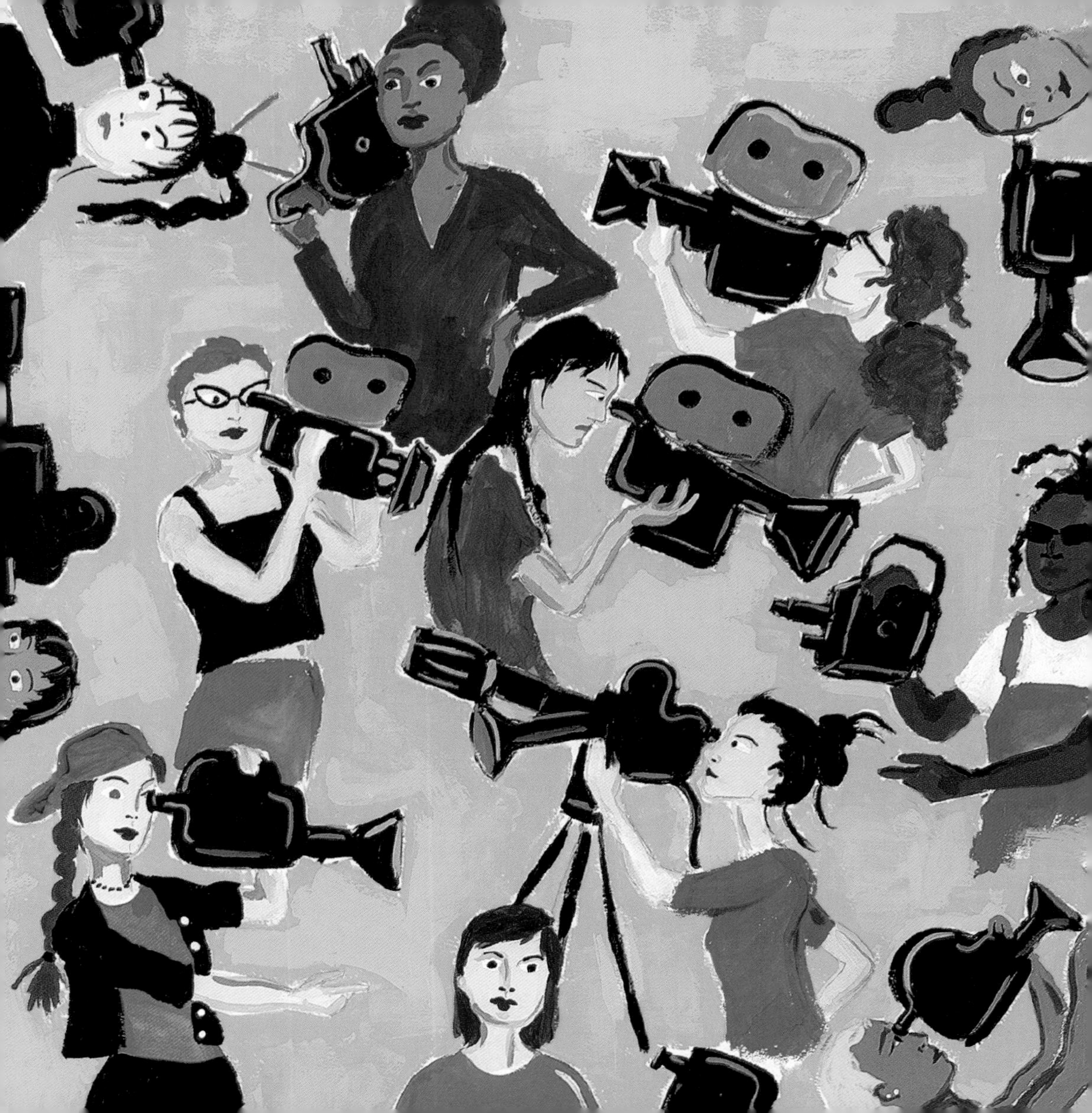

Self-Directed

Self-Discovery

BY LOUISA ERMELINO

"Incessantly, eternally make new roads wherever they may lead." —FYODOR DOSTOYEVSKY

As a girl growing up in Little Italy, a New York neighborhood as insular as any village in the Mezzogiorno, finding yourself was a tricky enterprise. Little girls were adored, but for their cuteness, sweetness, and pliability, and mostly as adjuncts to their brothers. A woman producing girl babies was inevitably kept pregnant. A boy the first time out was lotto; a girl next or somewhere in the mix was nice, but not—please understand—necessary, except maybe for those fathers who got teary at the thought of dancing to "Daddy's Little Girl" at the wedding. "Oh, you're finished," the other women would say to their lucky compatriot who had produced the magic duo.

Remember, in *The Godfather,* when Luca Brasi pays tribute to Don Corleone at the wedding of his daughter with the words, "And may their first child be a masculine child"? Well, my mother was next to Luca nodding her head yes.

My lucky Mom already had her male child when I was born which, it turned out, was also lucky for me. The resident boy-son-brother was everybody's primary concern. No one paid too much attention to my antics. And so no one was looking when I stepped off the path.

While the novel I wrote at eight went unread, my father did buy me a pink Smith-Corona portable typewriter to write it on. When I decided to go away to college and study engineering, my parents most certainly paid the tuition. And when I left for Europe and India and parts unknown, they were certainly nonjudgmental. Out of a combination of love, faith, and preoccupation with my brother, they certainly let me go my own way, left me to find myself.

I can say from the vantage point of middle age that experience and accomplishment contribute to self-worth, but so does being left alone, ignored in a positive sense. There's a lot to be said for finding nurture in the culture at large—and for getting by with a little help from your friends.

We start off looking through a pane of glass at the world, and then the rules start. The maps are drawn. Pretty soon we can't see through the window anymore; our vision stops right there. Get off the straight and narrow, it's too crowded, a subway car at rush hour. And when you're in that subway car, read the poems, like the one by Gertrude Stein: "I am Rose my eyes are blue/I am Rose and who are you/I am Rose and when I sing/I am Rose like anything."

Inspiration is everywhere. But when you find the secret to losing those ten pounds, keep it to yourself.

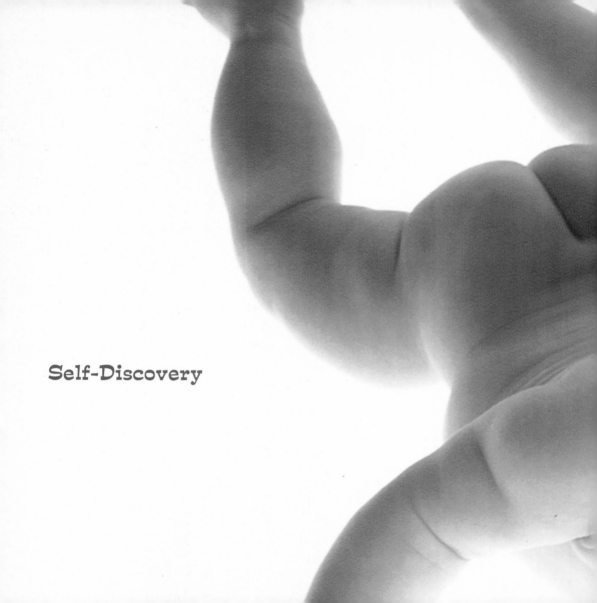

Self-Discovery

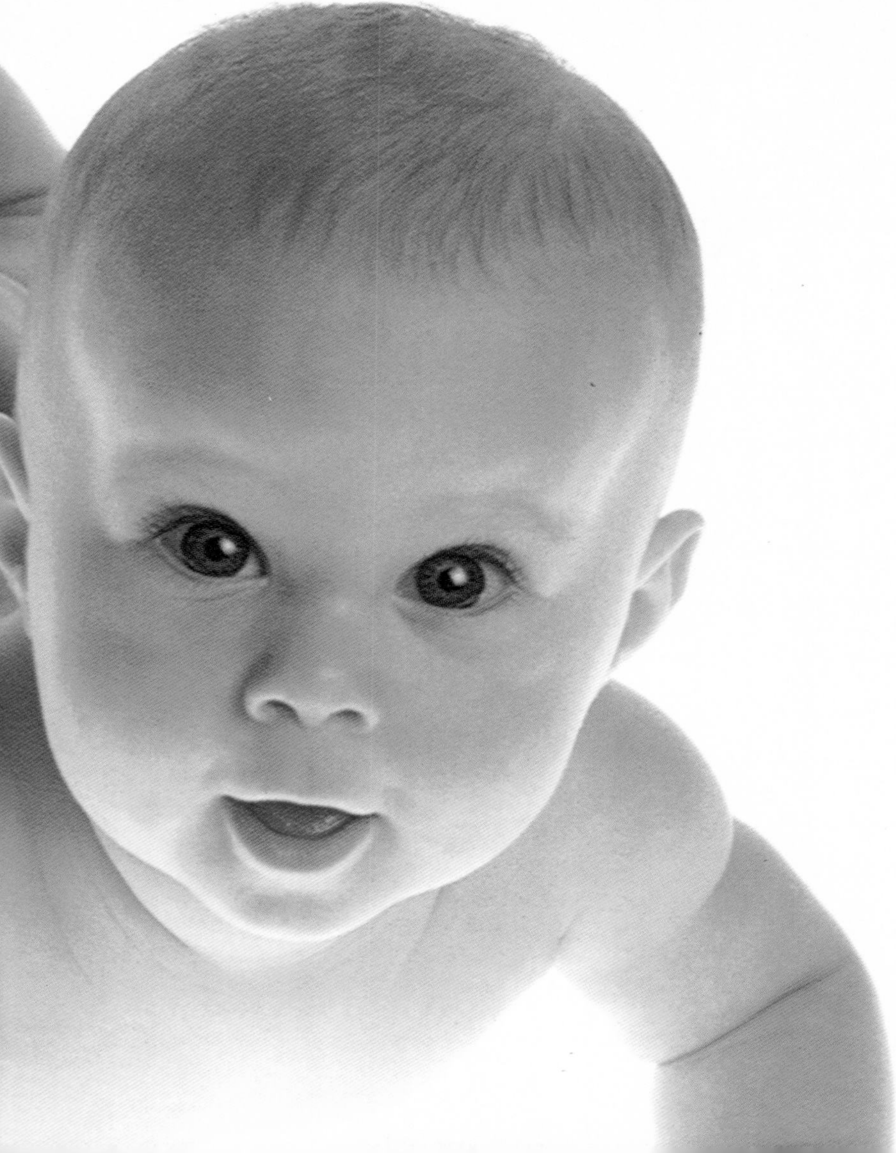

PENNY GENTIEU

SELF-DISCOVERY

*"How many cares
one decides
but to be someone."*

one loses when

not to be something,

—*Coco Chanel*

Self-Doubt

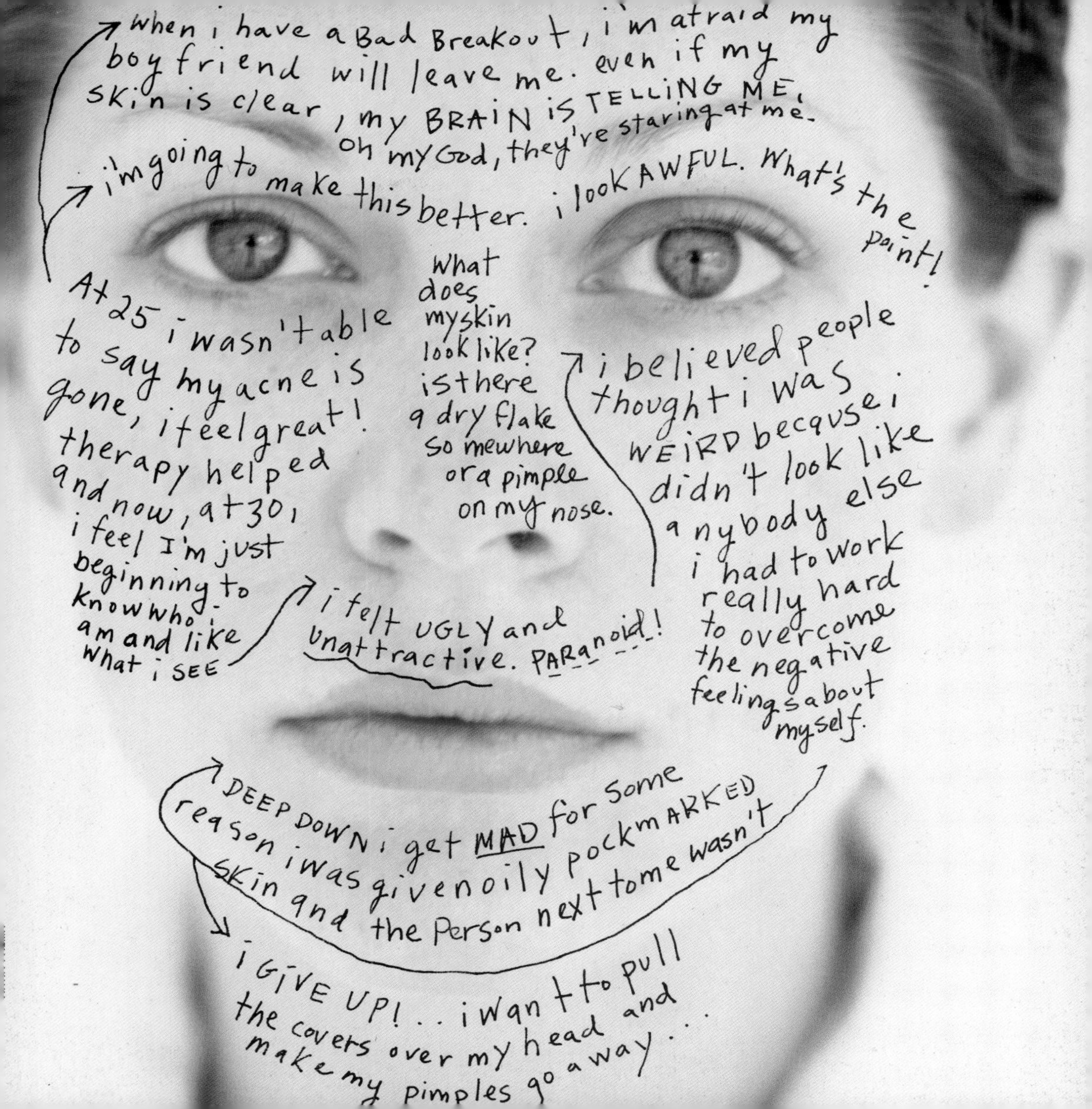
when i have a Bad Breakout, i'm afraid my boyfriend will leave me. even if my skin is clear, my BRAIN IS TELLING ME, oh my God, they're staring at me.
i'm going to make this better. i look AWFUL. What's the point!
What does my skin look like? is there a dry flake somewhere or a pimple on my nose.
At 25 i wasn't able to say my acne is gone, i feel great! therapy helped and now, at 30, i feel I'm just beginning to know who i am and like what i see
i believed people thought i was WEIRD because i didn't look like anybody else
i had to work really hard to overcome the negative feelings about myself.
i felt UGLY and unattractive. PARanoid!
DEEP DOWN i get MAD for some reason i was given oily pockmARKED skin and the Person next to me wasn't
i GIVE UP! .. i want to pull the covers over my head and make my pimples go away..

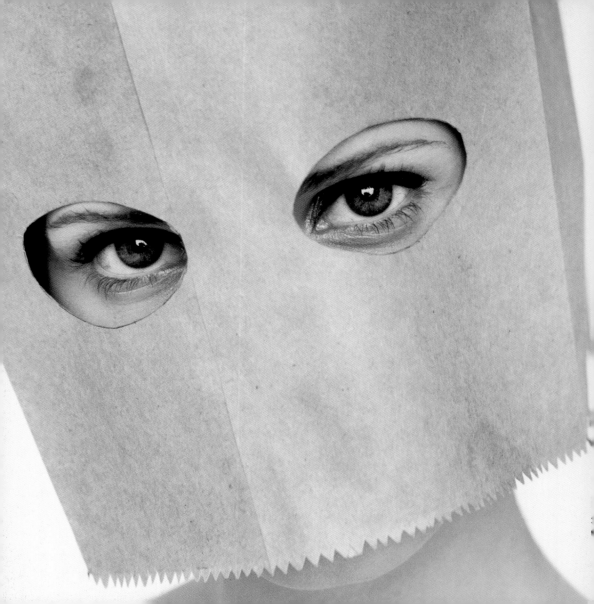

SELF-EFFACING

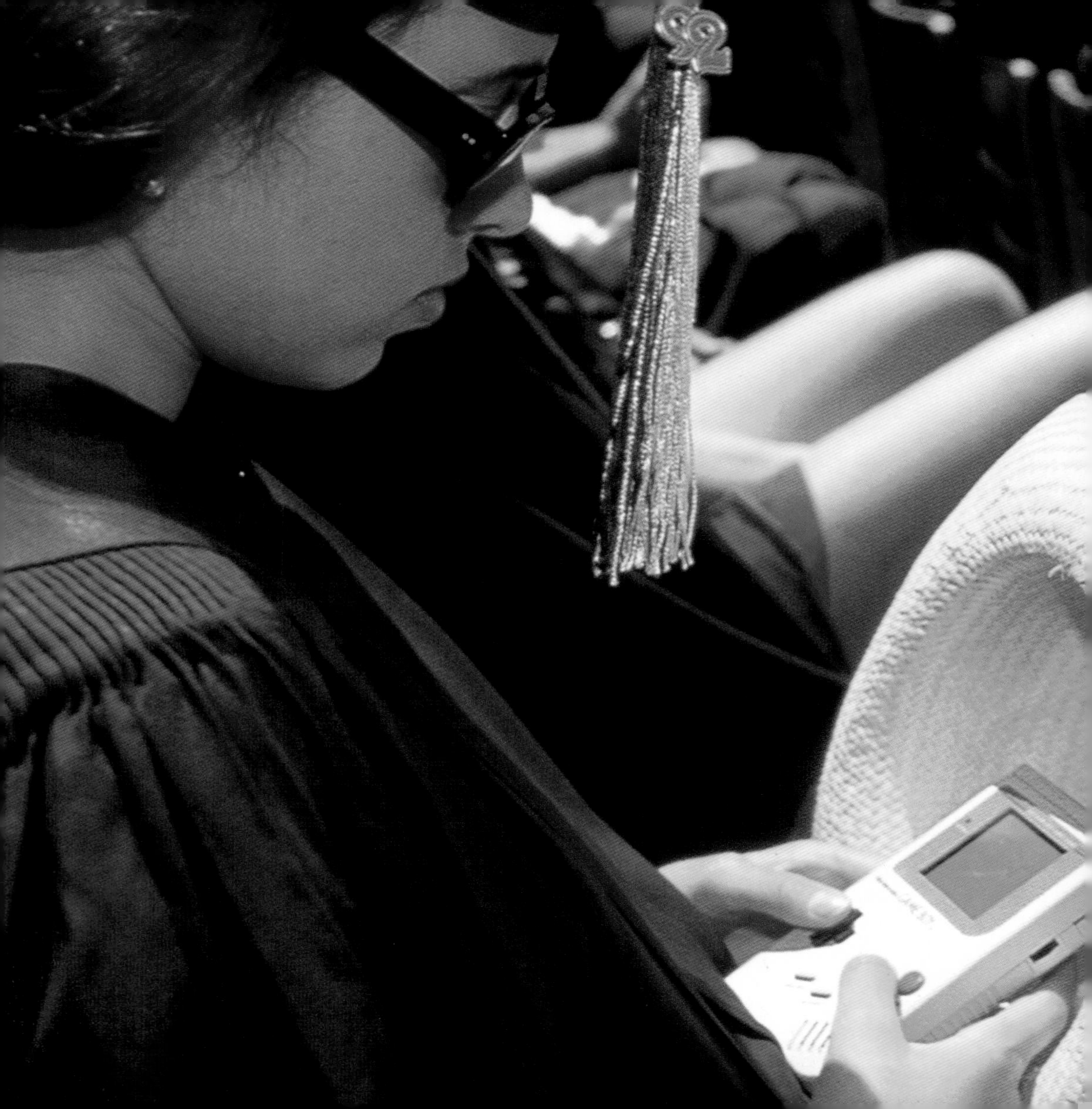

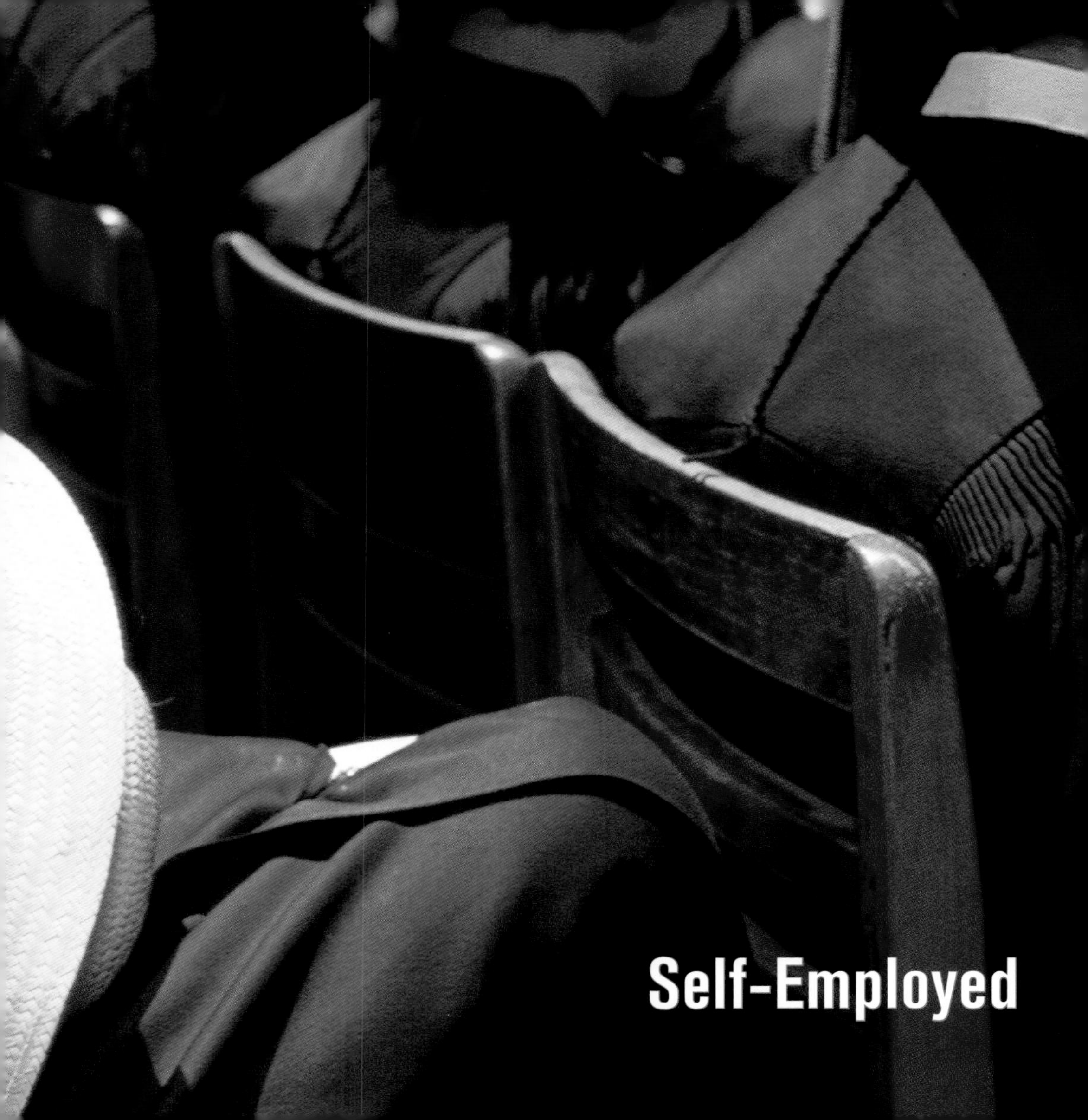

Self-Employed

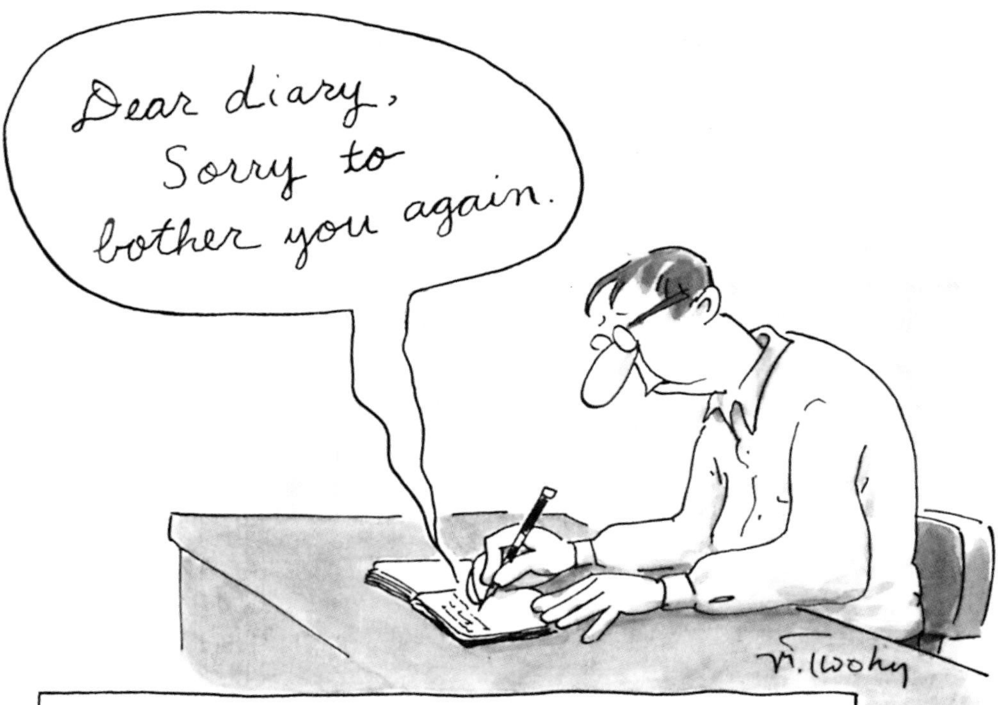
Dear diary,
Sorry to
bother you again.

LOW SELF-ESTEEM

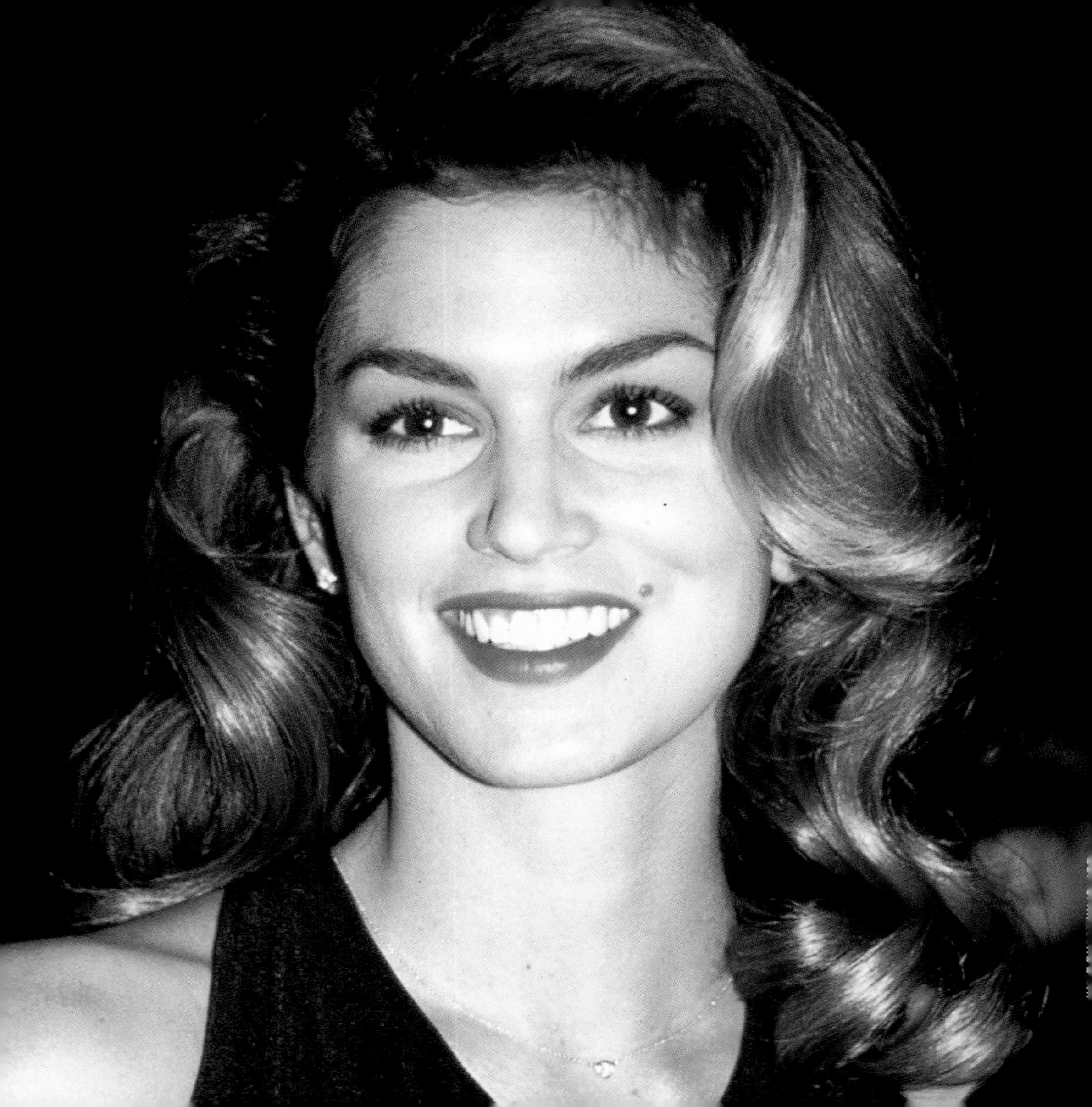

Self-Esteem

"For me, self-esteem has been the pursuit
of trying to listen to my inner voice and
trusting that only I know what feels right to
me . . . even if no one else understands a
certain decision. Having conviction in your
decisions gives you the confidence to live
with them." —Cindy Crawford

Self-Esteem

Self-esteem is hot steam from inside.

Mackenzie, age 6
Girls Inc. of Concord, NH

I'm the type of girl who will never ever keep my head down. I'm not a rich person or a poor person, but I'm what God made me and gave me: a voice, an artist, a poet, a good person, a good friend, and a great daughter.

Sasha, age 16
Girls Inc. of Holyoke, MA

I am smart, talented, and I can fold my body into the letter O.

Shannon, age 9
Girls Inc. of Pittsfield, MA

Self-esteem is how you feel about yourself. You can't lose your self-esteem; it's always there, but it could be BIG or very little. You can get a low self-esteem if you don't believe in yourself.

Kayla, age 12
Girls Inc. of Dothan, AL

I like me because I am me.
Raven, age 7
Girls Inc. of Greater Lowell, MA

Self-esteem is all involved in how you feel about yourself.
S ophisticated
E ducation
L ike everything about yourself
F orget about what others say
E xcited to be you
S elf-confident
T alking to other people
E veryone's associate
E steem is low or high
M aturity

Kagney, age 12
Girls Inc. of Wilmington, NC

79

self-esteem

GIFTS FROM THE
HOUSE OF LOW GOALS

T-Shirts

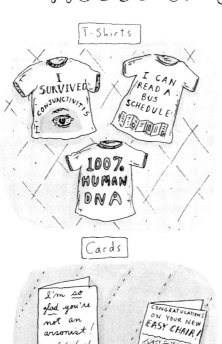

I SURVIVED CONJUNCTIVITIS

I CAN READ A BUS SCHEDULE

100% HUMAN DNA

Special-Occasion Cakes

WOW! ONLY 6 CAVITIES!

HAPPY TATTOO REMOVAL!

NO LOITERING ARRESTS IN ONE YEAR!

Cards

I'm so glad you're not an arsonist!

CONGRATULATIONS ON YOUR NEW EASY CHAIR!

Trophies

PARTICIPANT

R. Ch~

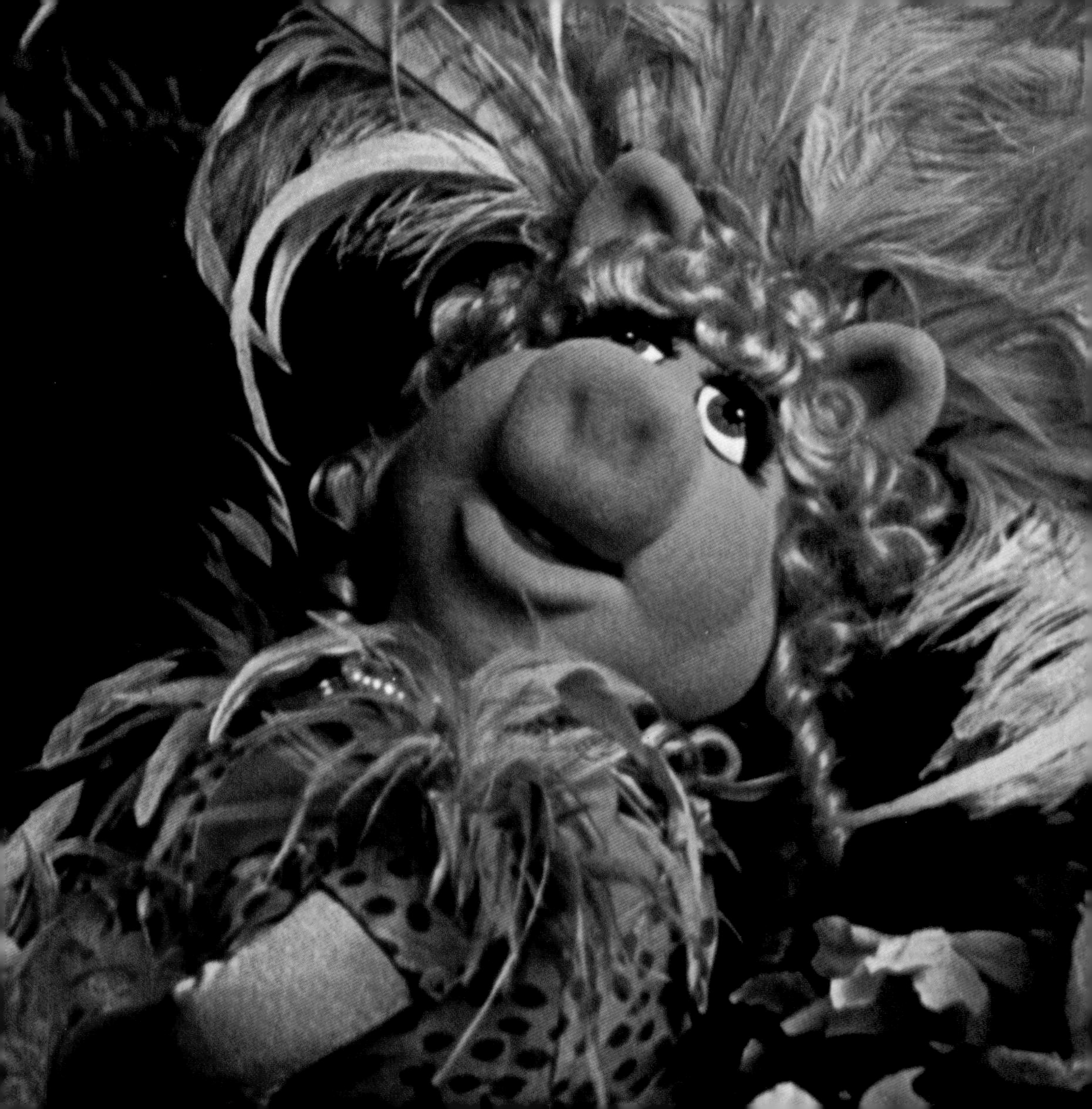

Self-Esteem

"If there's one thing *moi* has learned through the years, it's that true beauty comes from within. Inner pride and self-esteem do more for a woman than any cosmetic ever made—and they don't take an hour to put on in the morning."

—*Miss Piggy*

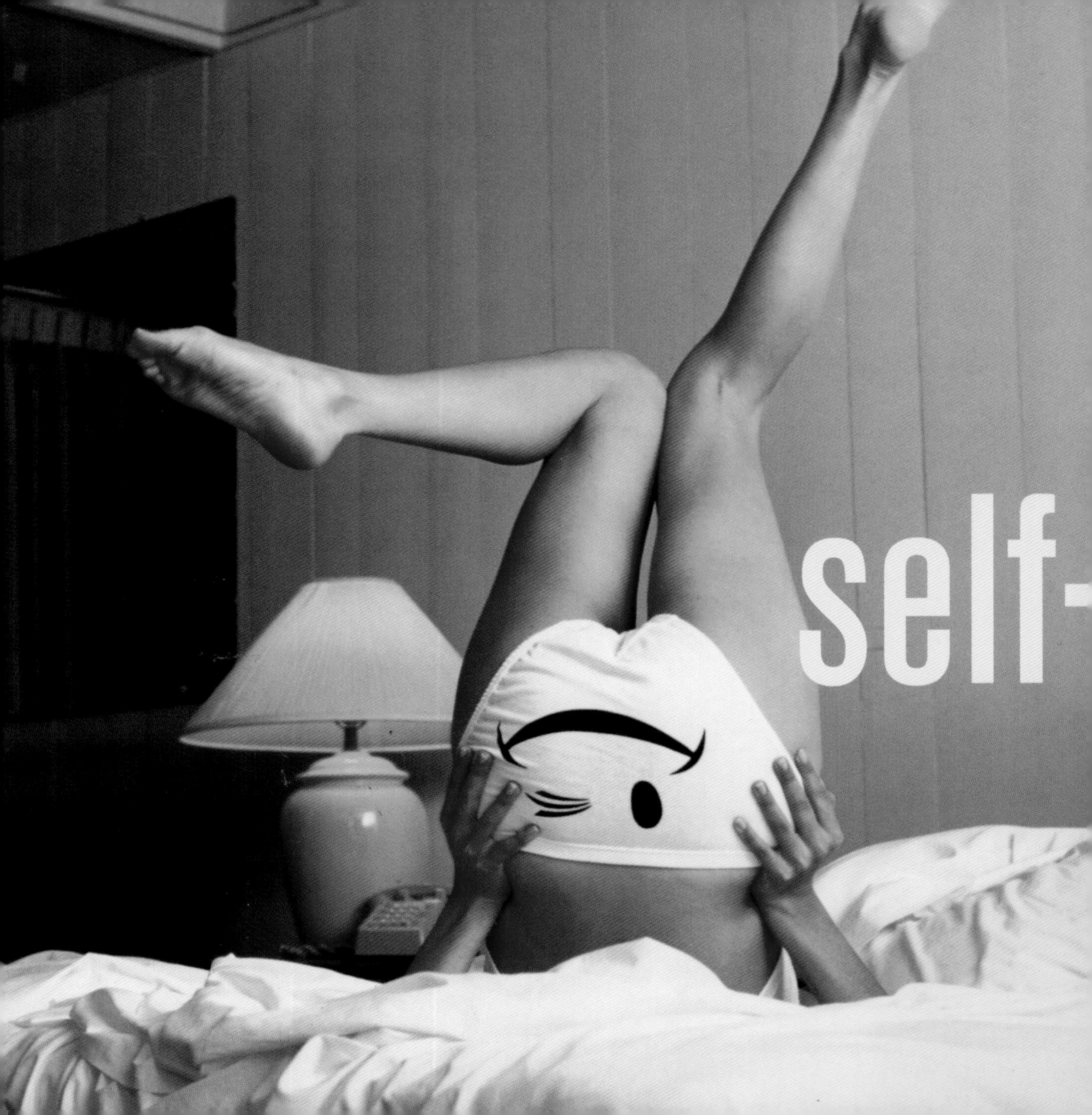
self-

exposure

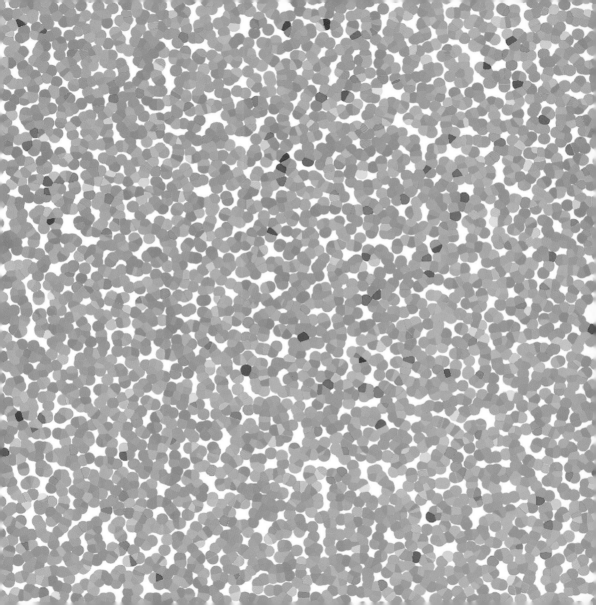

Self-Expression

Your voice is the soundtrack of your personality, as revealing as a Rorschach and as individual as a fingerprint. Letting it out can be like taking your emotional clothes off—one reason why so many of us refuse to allow our real voice to be heard. That is why people sometimes become mute after a horrific event happens to them. To protect their souls, they must hold the words deep inside.

The violation of the real voice often begins, sadly, in the classroom. Children learn that the writer's voice is different from the voice they use every day—different and superior. Eventually, as we grow older, something deeper and more troubling than the thought our spoken sentences do not parse makes us keep our voice inside our heart, like a genie in a lamp. We begin to use universal slang, psychobabble, and catchphrases to homogenize our voice, lest it seem different, inadequate, or too revealing of our thoughts and feelings. In *Annie Hall* when Woody Allen and Diane Keaton sit down to talk for the first time, we hear the words they speak and then the real words they're thinking, like subtitles on the screen. One is the societally correct voice; the second speaks from their real selves. This is the voice we cry with, rage with, and hear in our own heads.

It is difficult to let that voice out. But it is the only new thing you bring to the table when you write or talk; your personality—and therefore your voice—is different from that of anyone else in the world. That is why people still write books even though all the great themes were covered long ago. And it's why, timidly, tentatively, we still try to talk our own talk to the people we love.

—ANNA QUINDLEN

Speak up or you'll end

for yourself
up a rug.
—Mae West

self-generated

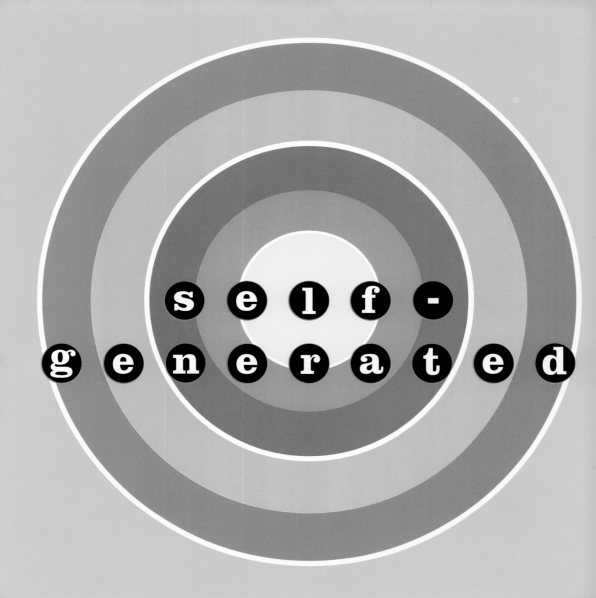

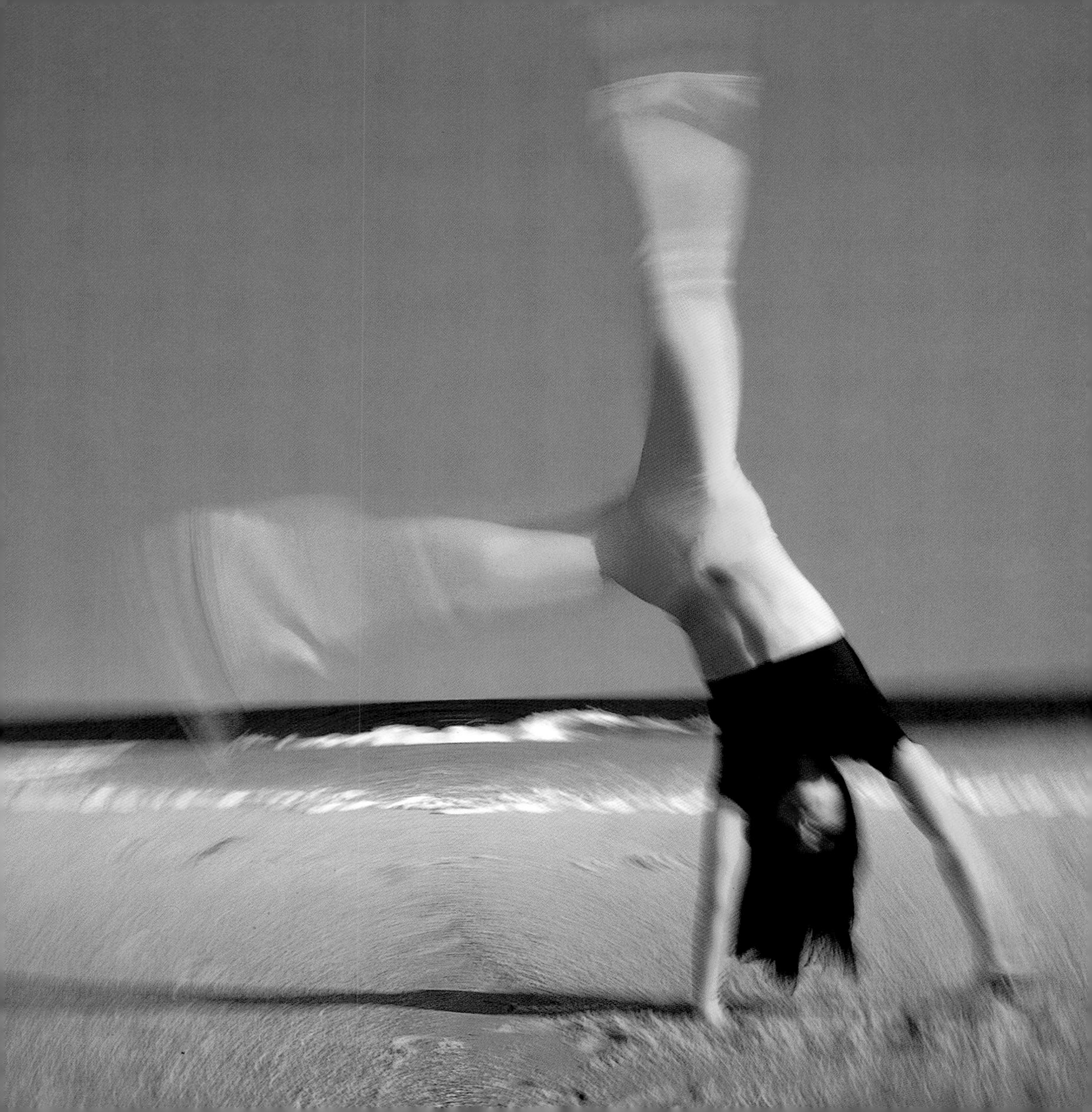

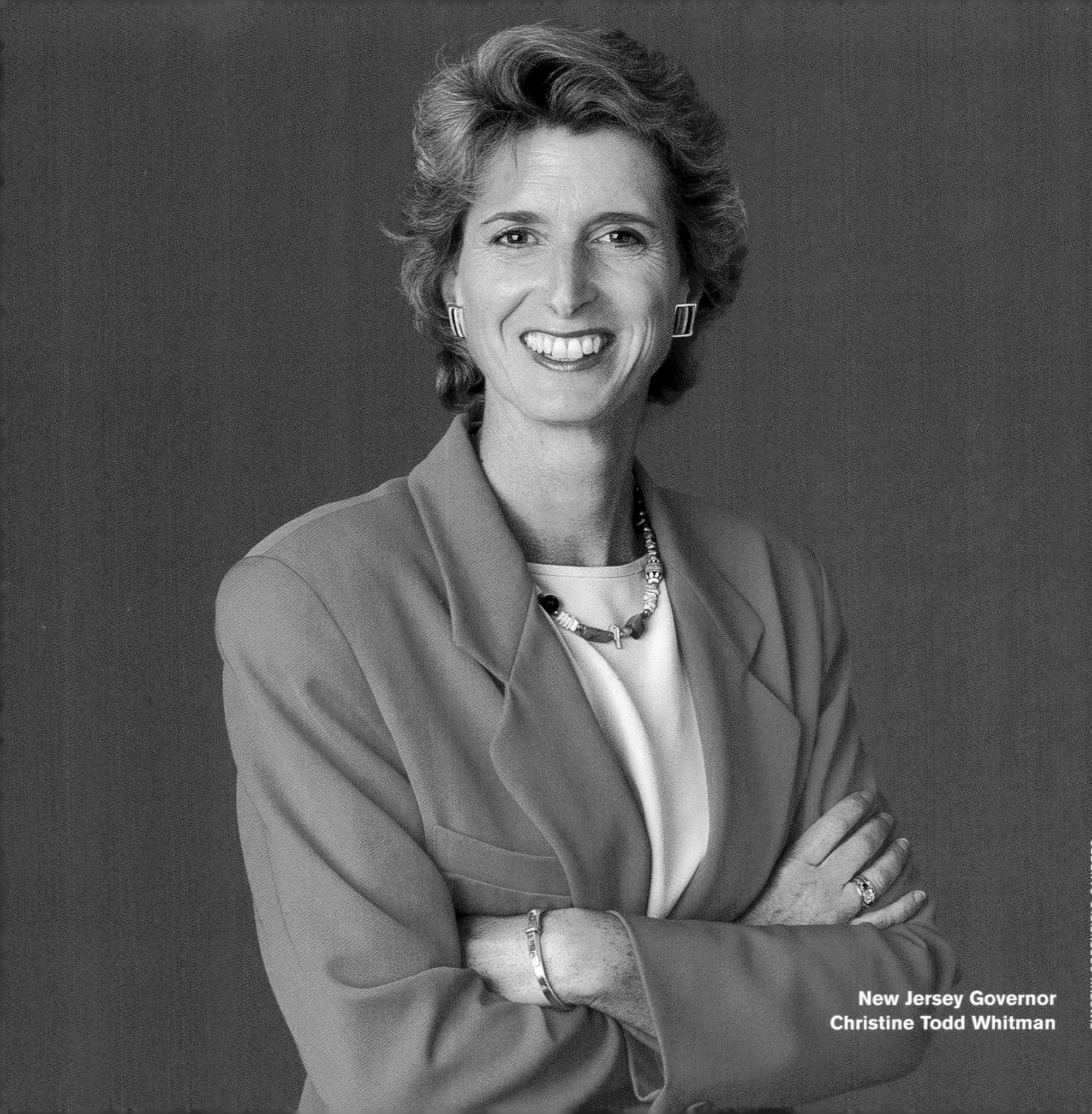

New Jersey Governor
Christine Todd Whitman

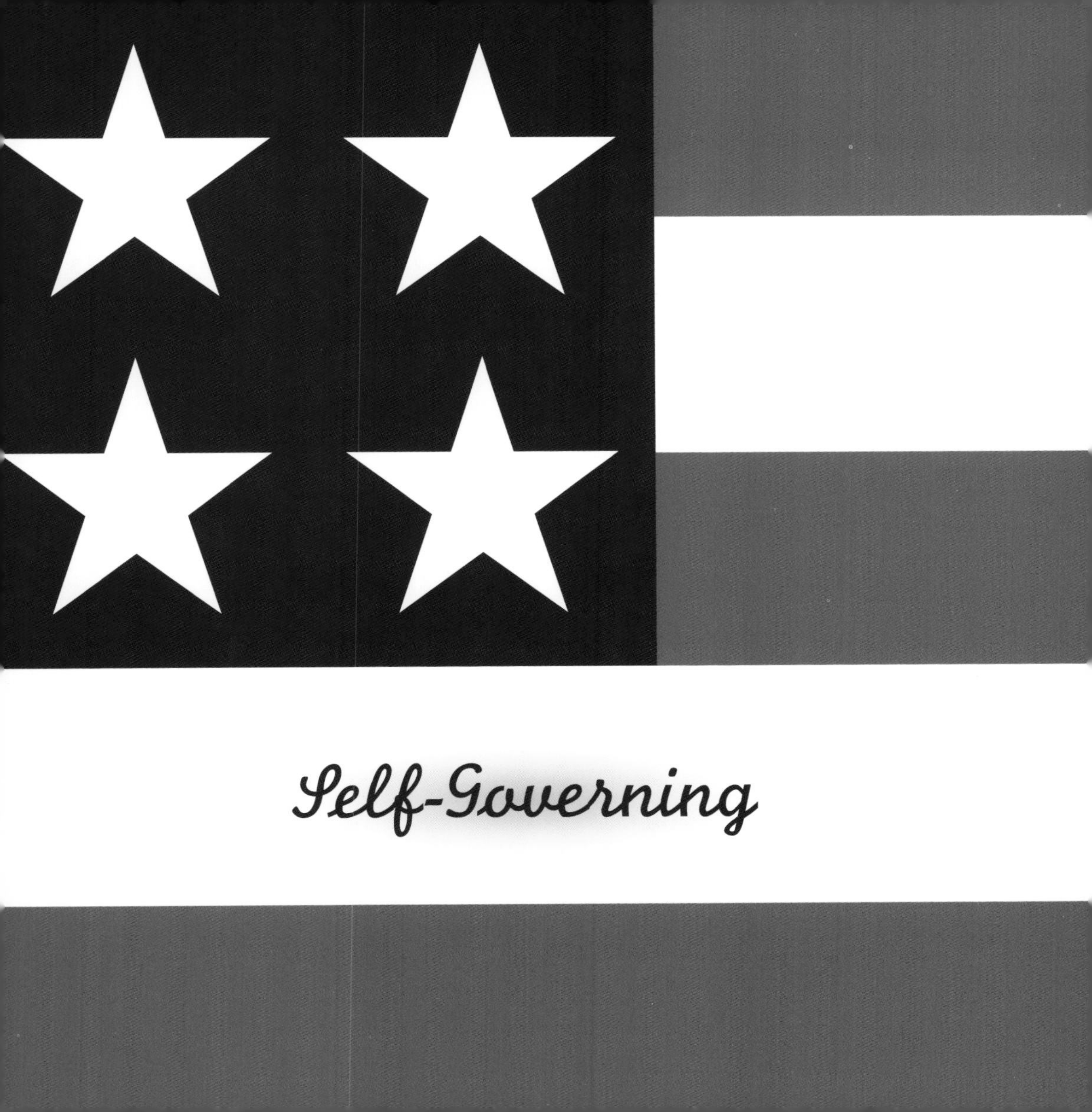
Self-Governing

Self-Healing

by Bernie S. Siegel, M.D.

I am a physician. Yet most of what I know about healing I learned not from medical school, but from the lives of the people I've met.

And the lesson has turned out to be surprisingly simple: You can't cure every disease, but every life can be healed.

Every day I meet people imprisoned in bodies and situations they cannot control, yet they live healed lives. A prisoner writes, "I used to get up each day condemned to die. Now I get up each day to live." He spends each day breaking concrete with a sledgehammer, but he has made a commitment to confront his fears, to battle for peace of mind.

Healing, then, is of the mind, not the body. But how do you heal your life when you have AIDS or cancer? The answer lies in living fully in the moment and letting your disease become your teacher. A Brothers Grimm parable I like tells of a genie in a bottle who is outsmarted by a brave young woman. After rebottling the wily genie, the woman decides to release him again and trust in her ability to deal with his unknown powers. In the end, he gives her a magic cloth that can turn metal into silver and heal all wounds. The young woman becomes one of the world's great healers.

Healing is a work of darkness. It happens when we go not east, west, north, or south, but in the fifth direction: inside. We can then turn to what frightens us—our genie—and say, "Why are you here? What can I learn from you? Why do you threaten me?" Then, as in the story of Job, "He delivers the afflicted by their afflictions, and opens their ears by adversity." Use your labor pains to give birth to a healed life, whether your "disease" is cancer, a bad relationship, or a dead-end job. Nothing is a match for your own inner strength.

Self-Help

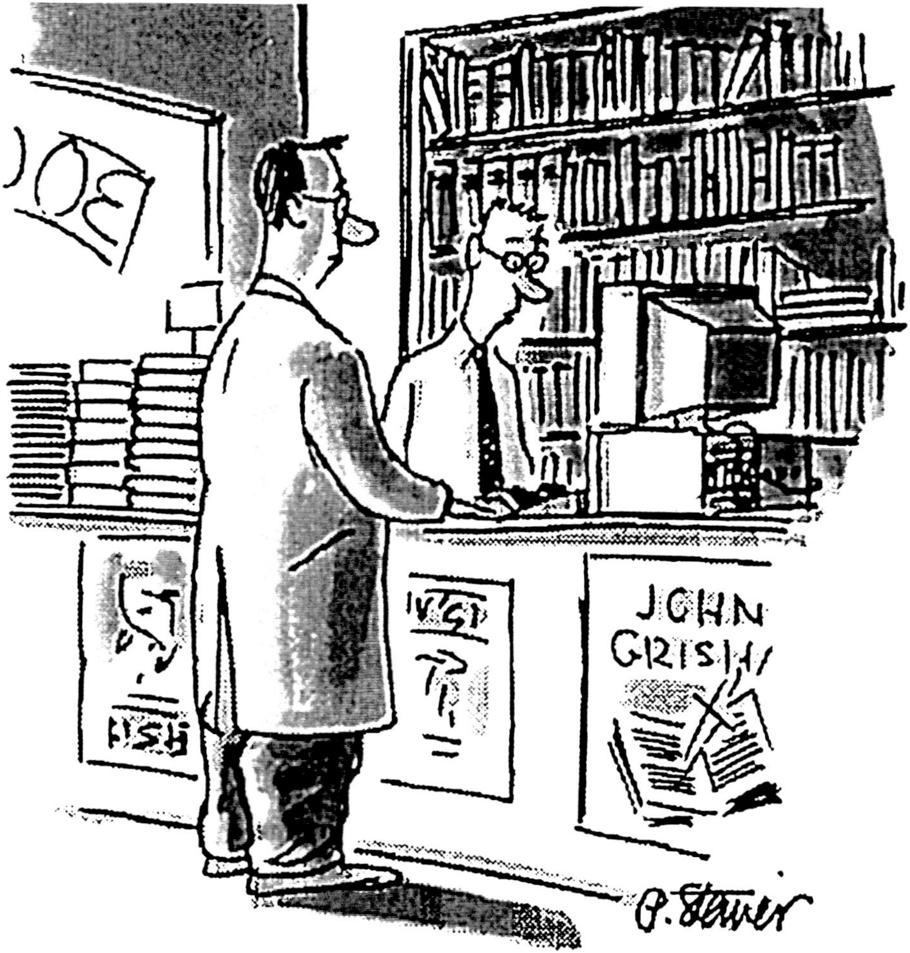
JOHN
GRISH

"The Bible... that would be under self-help."

SELF-HELP

by Elizabeth Berg

Recently I was browsing in a large bookstore, and found myself in the self-help section where I saw titles that addressed lowering stress, handling anxiety, raising self-esteem, learning optimism, managing mood, and more. Many more. Not far from a book on the need to find your soul mate was an equally authoritative text on why you should fully appreciate the joys of the single life. What's a pilgrim to think?

Actually, my problem with self-help books is that they encourage people not to think. They feed into the myth that there's a quick fix for everything, a one-size-fits-all solution to any problem. That's simply not true, and in our heart of hearts, we all know it. Nonetheless, many of us persist in looking for answers in the drive-through lane. It's just so appealing to think we can get away from doing work that takes time and effort and the kind of honesty that hurts.

After looking at all those self-help books, I needed a break. I looked in the poetry section at slim volumes capable of raising the hair on the back of your neck. I enjoyed paging through a book on cows, and a collection of short stories by Michael Byers that I'd read before but wanted to read from again. I ran my hands down the spines of art books the size of little doors, studied the sultry pictures of the French Quarter in the shiny-paged travel books on New Orleans. And I felt as if I could breathe again.

There are times in life when everyone needs a little help. Certainly a second opinion is a good thing to consider when one isn't sure which way to go. I myself am a big fan of the *I Ching*. But I worry that many readers of self-help books don't understand how much they already know, and that if they would give themselves their own psychic pickaxes they could uncover a lot of intuitive wisdom. Most of all, I worry that they'll spend too much time in the self-help section when the real cure might be in poetry.

When it comes to the things that matter most, there are never any shortcuts. To pretend that true enlightenment can be found between the covers of a self-help book is to do a terrible disservice to the unique makeup and abilities of most people. Nearly all of us can find some truth in the psychobabble that most self-help books are. But nearly all of us also have abilities that we never tap into, work that we can and must do by ourselves in order to scratch our greatest itch. It is our job to try to find the unique pegs that fit our own unique holes. And to remember that the operative word in self-help is *self.*

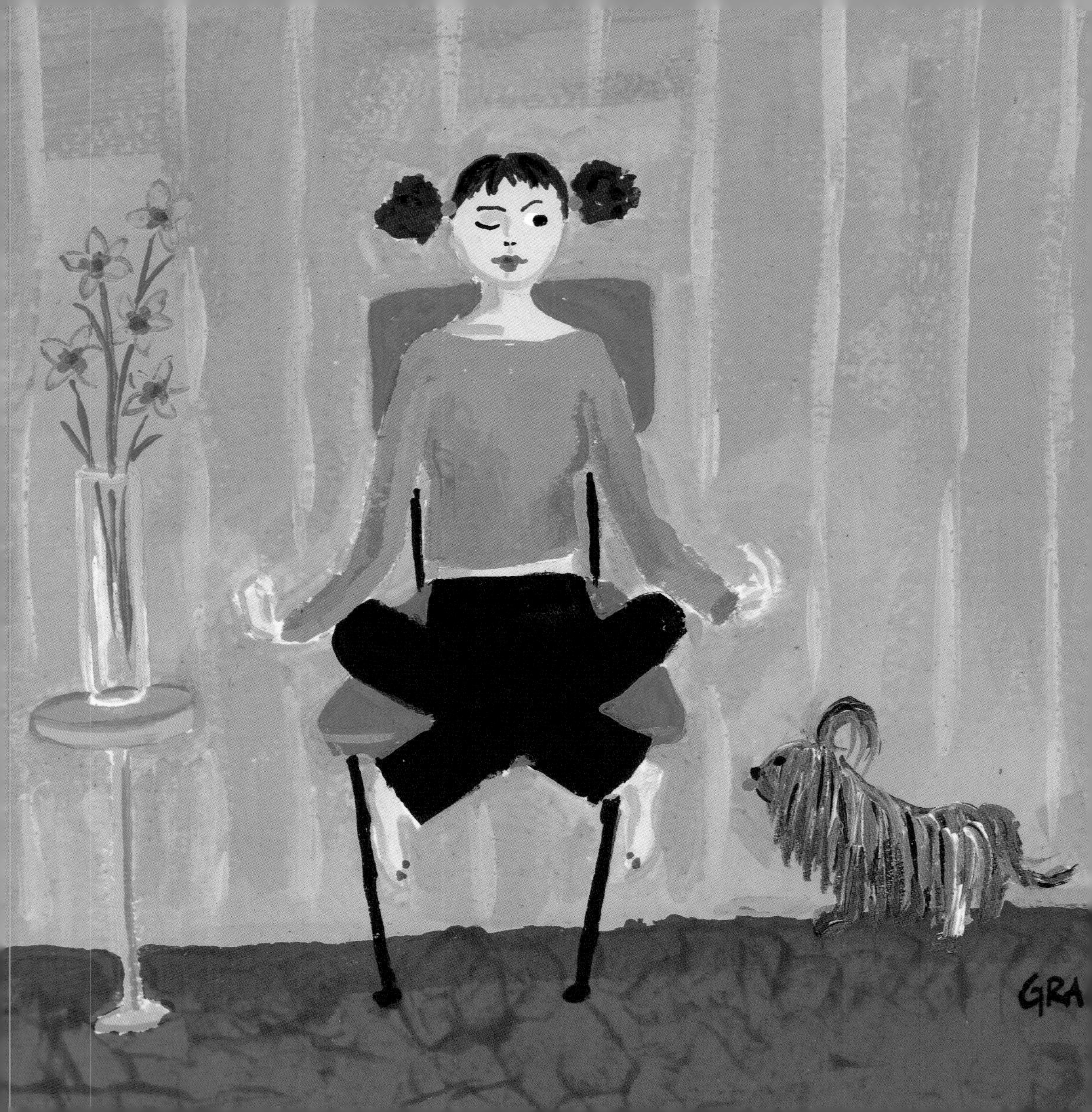
GRA

Self-Hypnosis

SELF-IDENTIFIED

SELF-PITY

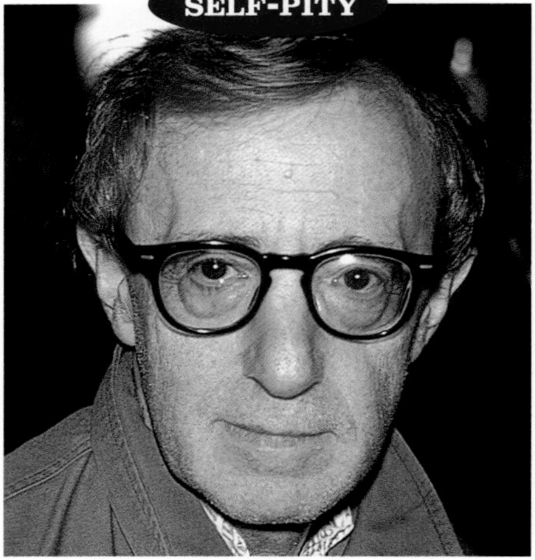

Woody Allen

SELF-PRODUCED

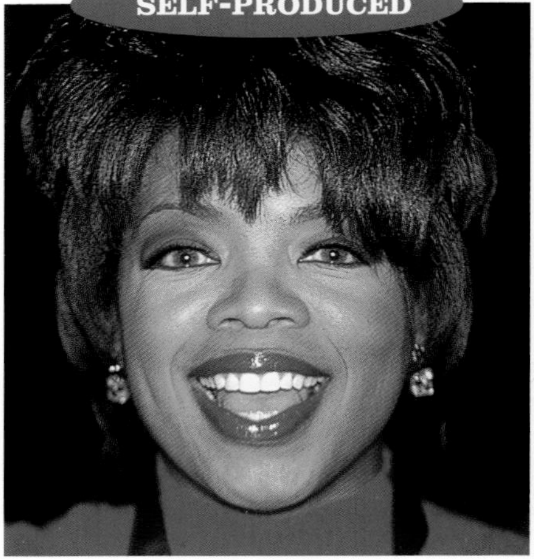

Oprah Winfrey

SELF-REPLICATING

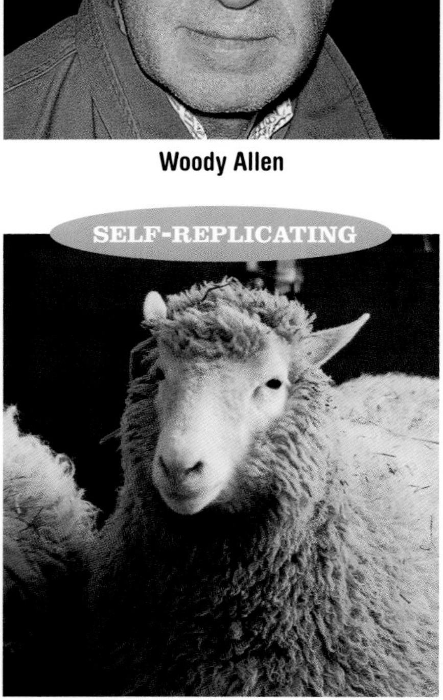

Dolly

SELF-EMPLOYED

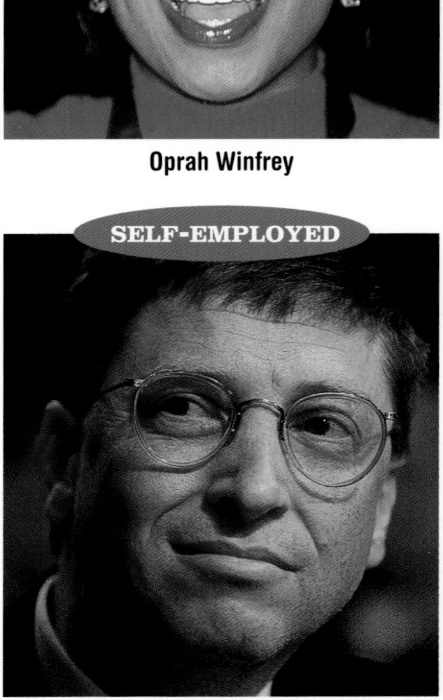

Bill Gates

ALLEN: GREGORY PACE/SYGMA; WINFREY: ANDREA RENAULT/GLOBE PHOTOS; DOLLY: N. POLAK/SYGMA; GATES: FICARA/SYGMA

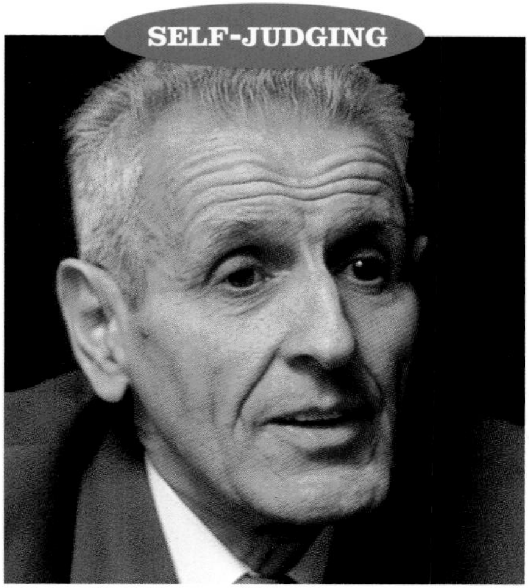
SELF-JUDGING

Jack Kevorkian

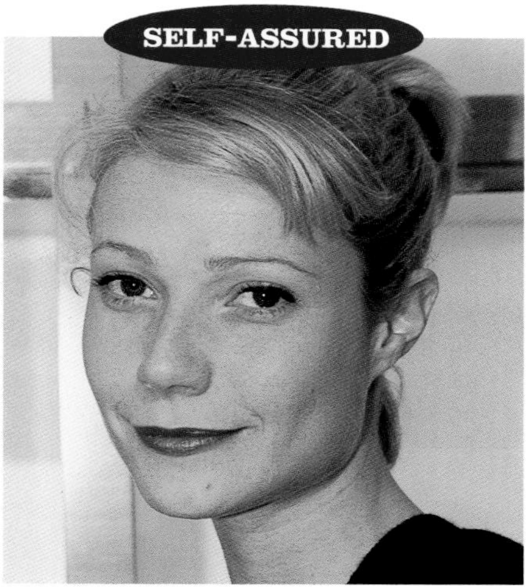
SELF-ASSURED

Gwyneth Paltrow

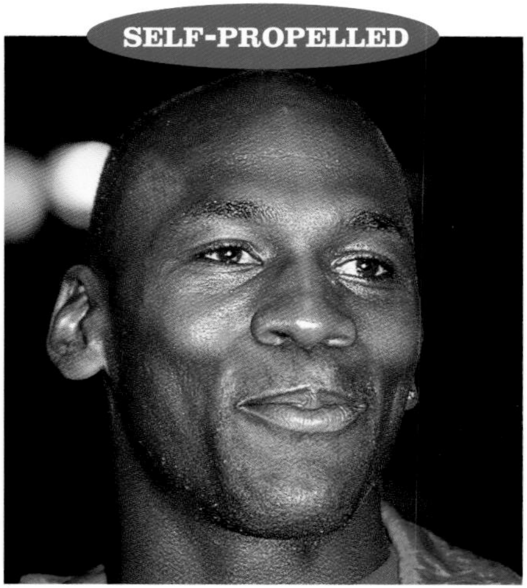
SELF-PROPELLED

Michael Jordan

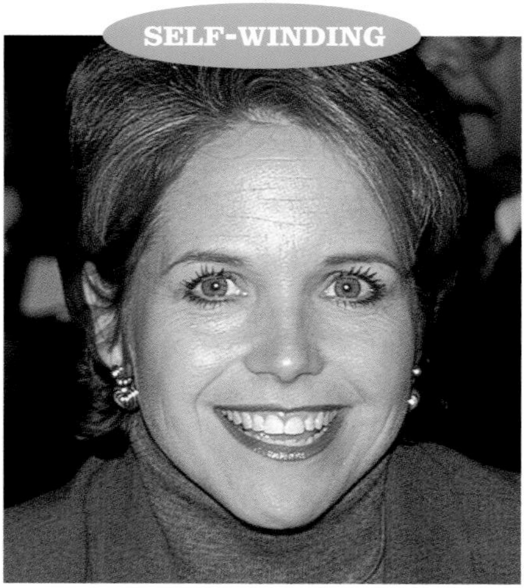
SELF-WINDING

Katie Couric

SELF-IDENTIFIED

SELF-LOATHING

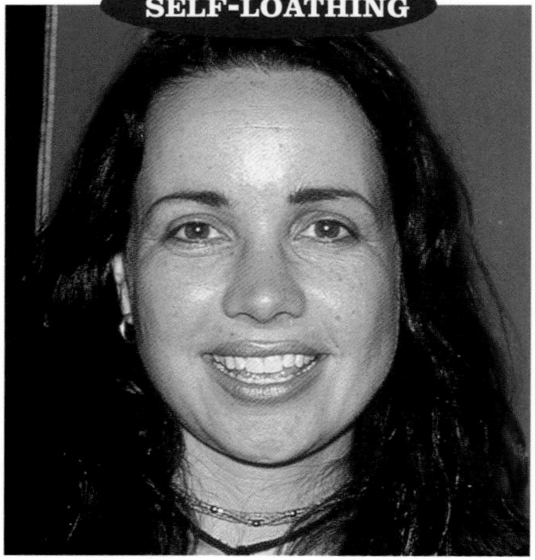

Janeane Garafalo

SELF-DIRECTED

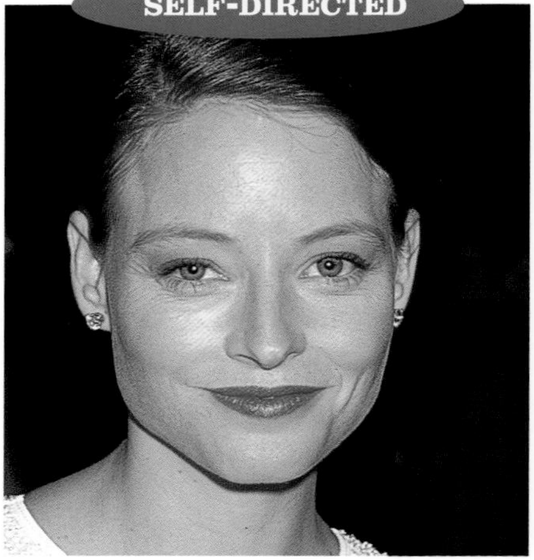

Jodie Foster

SELF-PLEASED

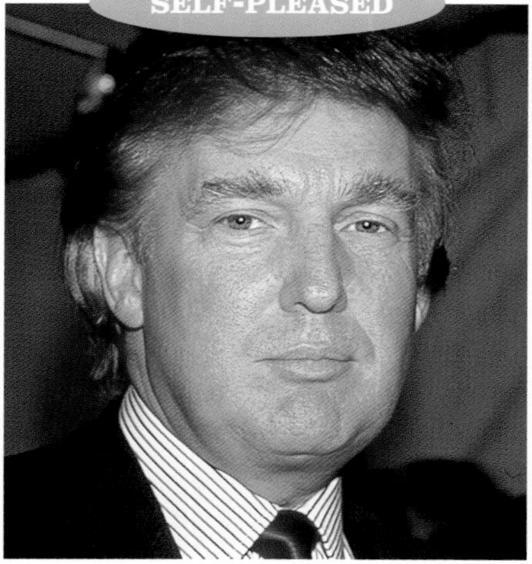

Donald Trump

SELF-SACRIFICE

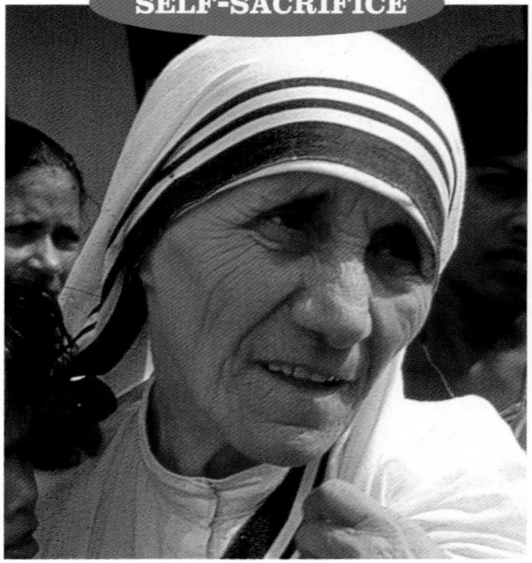

Mother Teresa

GARAFOLO: GREGORY PACE/SYGAM; FOSTER: LISA ROSE/GLOBE PHOTOS; TRUMP: ANDREA RENAULT/GLOBE PHOTOS; MOTHER TERESA: SYGMA

SELF-SCULPTED

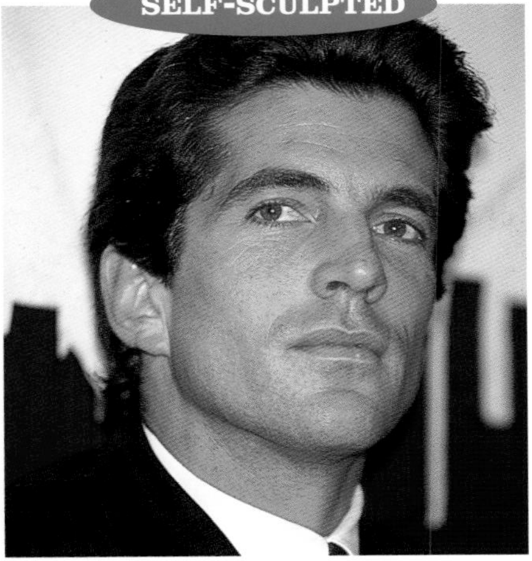

John F. Kennedy, Jr.

SELF-SAVING

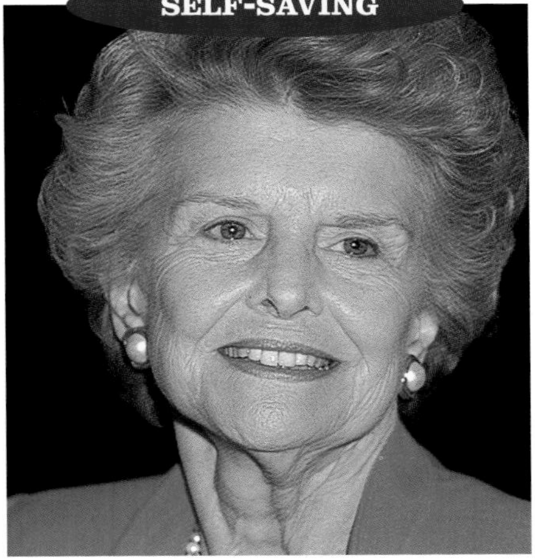

Betty Ford

SELF-DELUDED

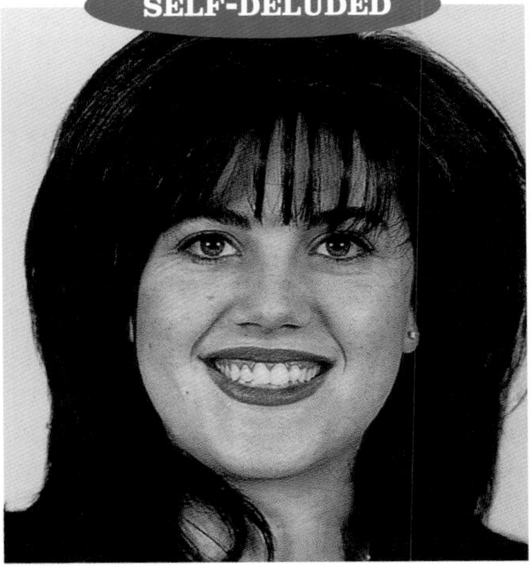

Monica Lewinsky

SELF-ABSORBED

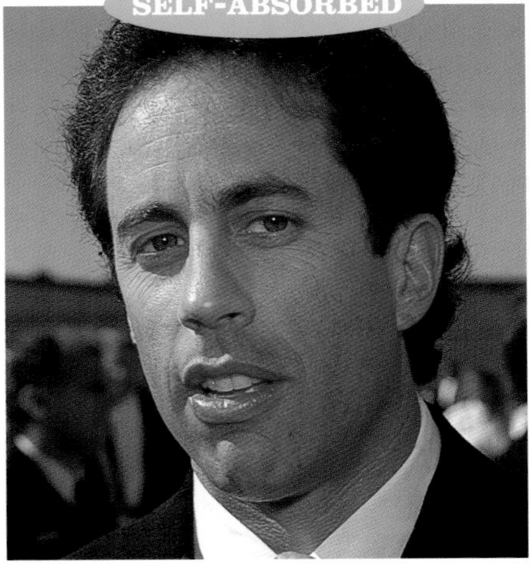

Jerry Seinfeld

Self-Image

An Interview with Lauren Hutton

Q: How has your self-image changed?

A: I prefer my pictures now. I don't put on just anything. I don't allow any styling, unless I like it. I look better now because I've grown into who I want to be. I'm no longer buffeted by the seas of fashion.

Q: How does a woman's self-image change as she gets older?

A: Until very recently in this country, our culture didn't provide us with strong images of women. Not many "she-heroes." We've always seen ourselves as a country of girls. And as soon as a girl became a woman, she had to leave the business of image-making.

But times are changing. Never again will girls be without a place to grow that is vital, sensual, powerful, and, hopefully, joyous. There's an important need in our culture to see women in this light. It's politically important. And part of the need is demographics; my generation, which grew up in "the sixties", has the most money and influence today.

Q: What's the most important lesson you've learned about the brevity of youth?

A: Models are always taught to look younger than they are. At my crisis, age 40, I was wearing ridiculous clothes because I was trying to look young. Now I wear minimal makeup, look my age and feel good about it. You must accept who you are. If you don't like who you are, you have to start making some brutal changes. See a therapist if it's hard to change on your own. Otherwise, how can you figure out what you want to do? And how can you be any good to anyone you love?

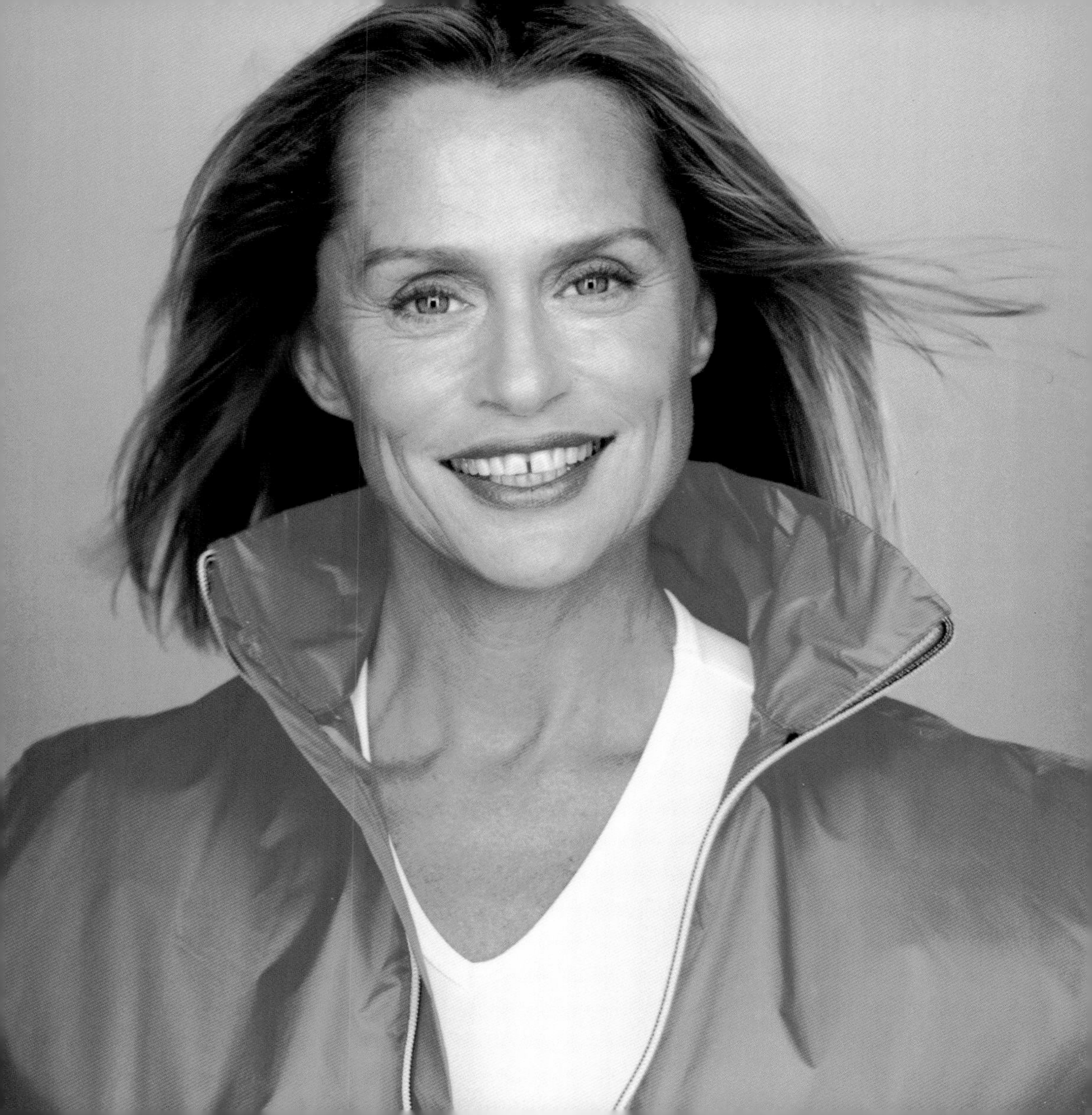

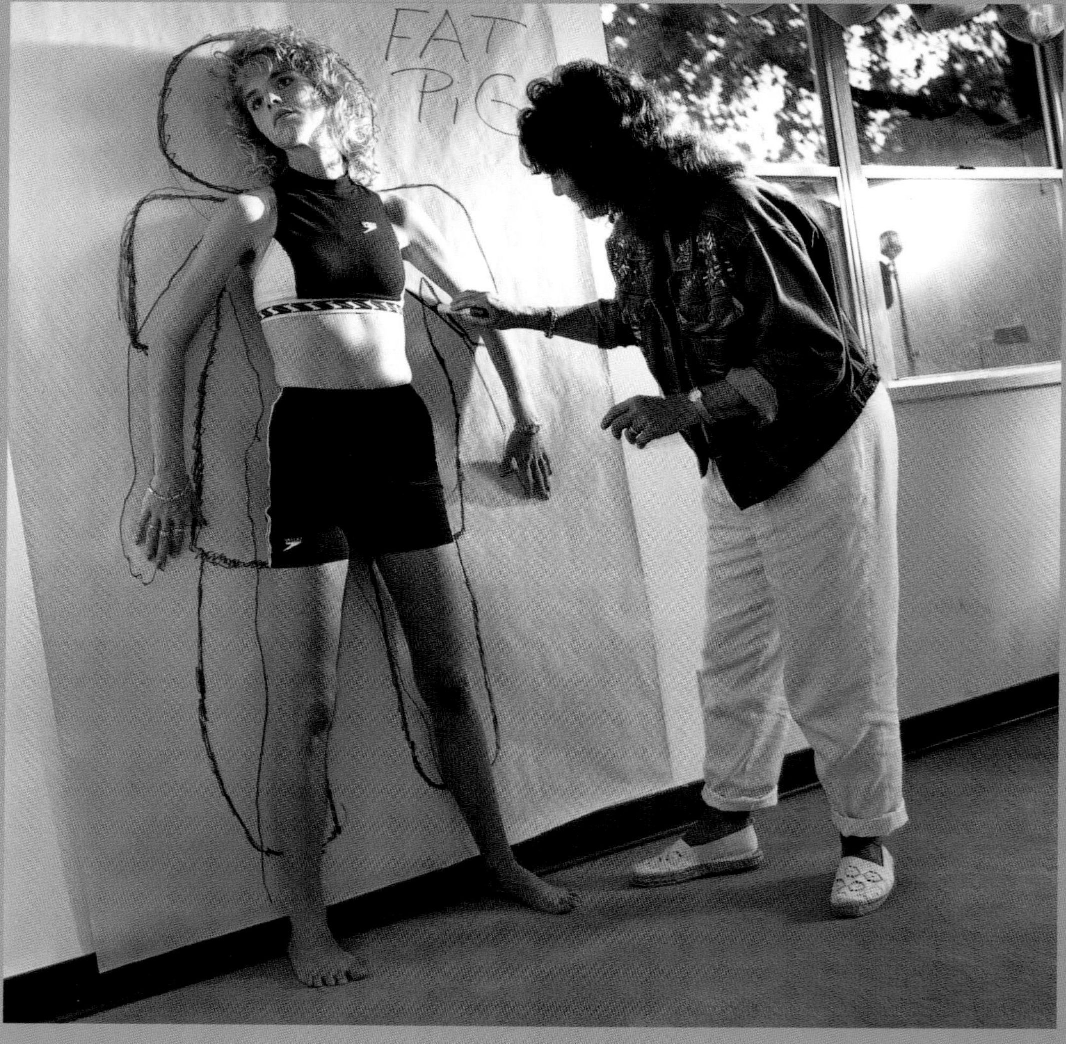
FAT
PiG

Self-Image

Mary Ellen Mark

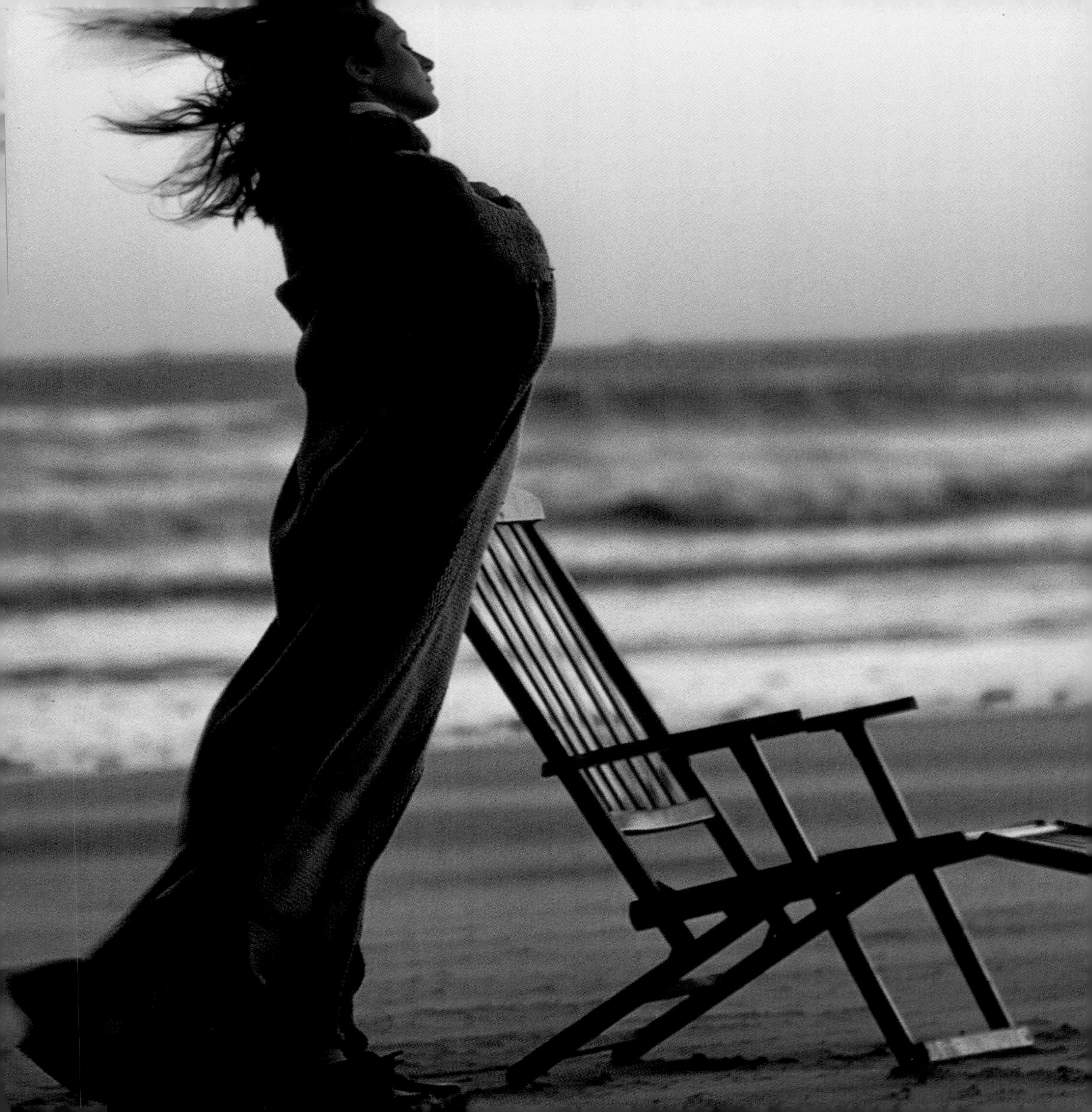

SELF-IMPOSED EXILE

BY ANNETTE O'TOOLE

From September 1, 1984, until June 23, 1998, I willingly put myself under house arrest in a beautiful little town in southern Oregon. With the determination of an inmate who decides to read every law book in the prison library and pass the bar from San Quentin, I set about becoming a housewife extraordinaire, figuring I already had a head start, being an experienced knitter and birthday-cake baker. I left L.A. with no regrets and the idealistic notion that I could commute to all my acting work from a place that had no direct flights to anywhere in the United States except Portland, Oregon. I did this because I wanted a "real" life with all my heart and because I thought if I connected the dots, I'd wind up with the perfect picture. But I think that only works if you're the one drawing the dots to begin with and if you don't confuse the words compromise and sacrifice.

So I had two babies, two miscarriages, a trembling marriage, lovely in-laws, PTA meetings, dinner (all food groups represented) on the table at 6 P.M., *Mystery!* on Thursday nights, and then, finally, my friend Joan.

It turned out that after my second daughter was born on the last day of 1987, I just couldn't maintain all my household duties and keep my hand in as an extremely demi Hollywood goddess. And since the cleanliness of the house was in direct correlation with

my husband's moods, it was decided that I should have some "help." So I reluctantly agreed to let a stranger come into my house once a week—a woman stranger, who was probably better at everything I was trying to do, with the exception of cold readings. But I had reached my limit of exhaustion and would do anything to stave off the specter of my Electrolux.

So Joan arrived at my own private Elba. And even though I had figured on being in solitary, Joan had a key to my cell that I didn't even know existed. She became a constant in my life, and week by week, year by year, a bond of love was formed that was all the stronger for its coming out of left field. We admired each other, our children played together, my eyes gradually opened to the heartbreaking truth of my situation, and the house was clean as a whistle, to boot! We just liked one another, is the thing.

When my beautiful paint-by-number picture finally and inevitably came crashing down, she was there to cry with me. And when I decided my time of exile was finally over, she hugged me and let me go.

Always follow your heart. But if it leads you to a far-off place and then deserts you there, don't panic. Just wait for a while. Help will find you if you want it to. And if you look in a place you might not expect—like in your shower stall, disguised as a woman scrubbing down the tiles with Lysol.

Self-Indulgence

Ben & Jerry's Mint with Oreo Cookies ice cream. Two pints, one spoon. The trick is to let the second pint defrost while you're eating the first one.

—Rosie O'Donnell

Milk chocolate. I don't like white chocolate because it tastes like vanilla to me.

—Gloria Estefan

I love desserts and bread and butter

—Elle McPherson

Liqueur-filled Swiss chocolates, stowed in my bag on return flights from Europe.

—Dr. Ruth Westheimer

Top of the list: pasta.

—Donald Trump

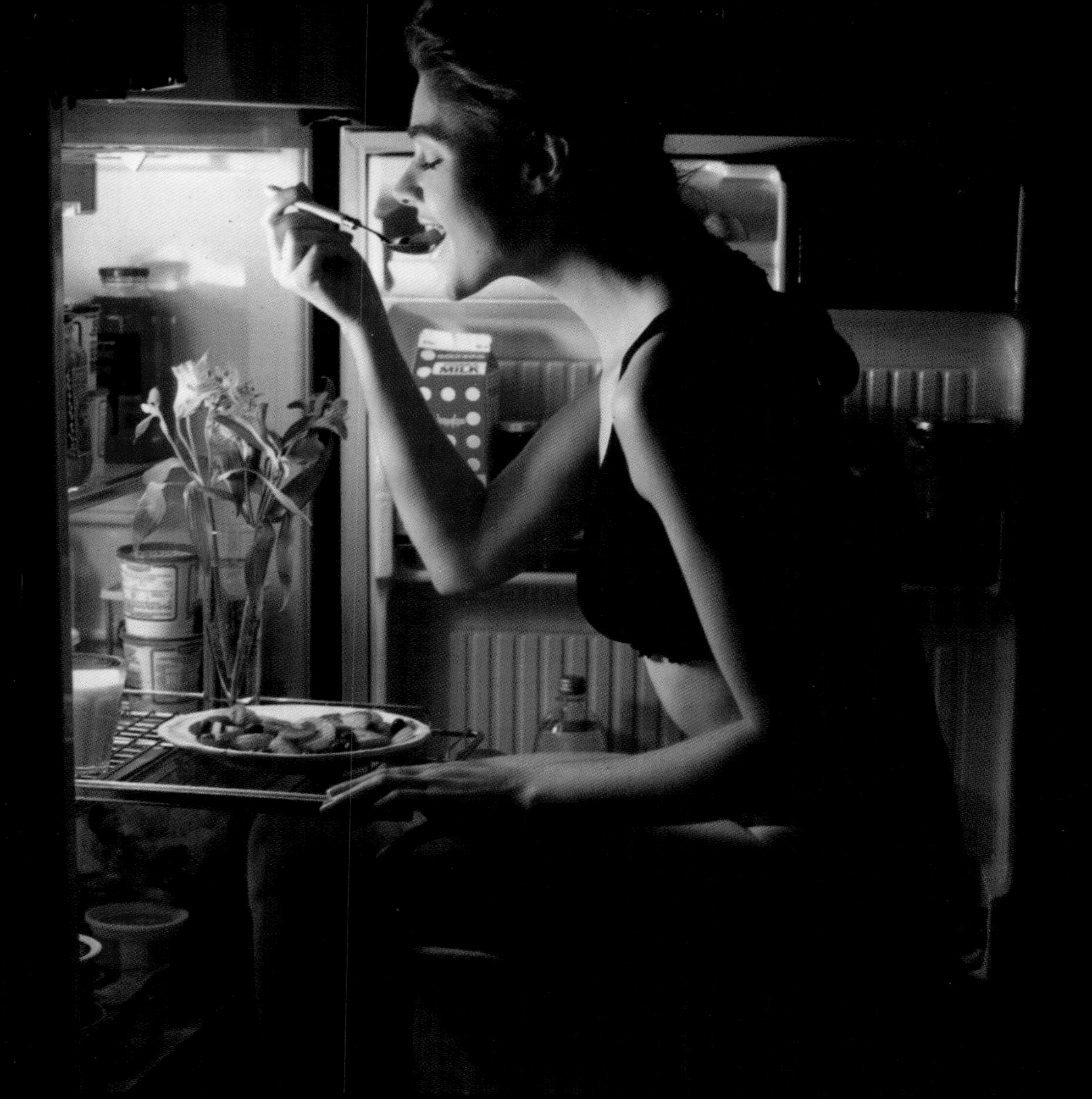
MILK

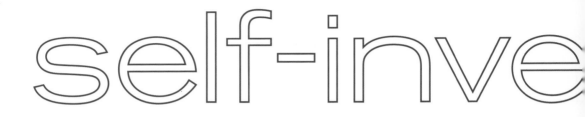

As Americans we've inherited the idea that you can make yourself over following whatever inspirational model you prefer. The history of this country is one of self-improvement, and self-improvement is, in turn, the twin of self-invention. The very country itself was designed to improve upon an older, dysfunctional European model.

The American westward expansion was made up of people leaving their old selves behind. People who were convicts and bootblacks in Europe reemerged as the new dancing masters and cooks. Others made fortunes in the business of helping people invent new selves. Courses in drawing and writing were advertised on matchbooks; so were ones in vocabulary improvement and charm. Arthur Murray dance classes! Learn to sew! Charles Atlas! Don't be a 97-pound weakling! Learn by correspondence! Go to night school! In this, the most industrious of industrialized nations, our role models were like Abe Lincoln: They burned the midnight oil, they trained, they consulted. There were elocution lessons. Brunettes became blondes.

But the word *self-invented* and the idea of self-invention have rather unfairly taken on a negative connotation in the twentieth century, as if they were the oppo-

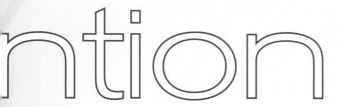

by Diane Johnson

site of *authentic* and *sincere.* Could this be the work of the psychological theories of the new age? People are no longer being asked what they could be; they are asked to ascertain what they already are. All that time and money to find out who you already are means you have a certain investment in that person. Now you are less willing to change. "Let me tell you who I *am,*" we've learned to say.

But in a paradoxical way, self-discovery is the enemy of self-invention, and a way of being stuck. If we are too enamored of who we are, too invested in it, we can't move on.

Of course, self-knowledge is valuable to self-invention: I must recognize that I am timid and lazy before I can summon the resolve to be bold and energetic. You have to know what you are combating. But then, the self once known, the sky should be the limit. Think big. As Americans we've inherited a lot of bracing slogans to face the future with, and most of them do encourage us to transcend our workaday selves, grow, accomplish, buff. We can invent ourselves–again!–and in the process of self-invention, we can discover self-satisfaction.

Self-Involved

by Marion Winik

If yours is not a story that interests you,
it can hardly be expected to keep a dinner companion alert.

Any 12-year-old girl who reads her teen magazines can tell you that if you don't love yourself, no one else can love you, either. I move to expand this thought: Love is not enough. Self-involvement is key. If you're not involved with yourself, no one will be involved with you.

I mean, really.

If you're not interesting enough to get and keep your own attention, how can you possibly expect to entertain anyone else for the length of a meal, much less a lifetime? What you want. What you need. What inspiring opportunities arise and cruel obstacles impinge. What crises erupt and decisions eventuate from the moment your eyelids flutter open until the hour you put on your black satin blindfold to make it all go away. If this is not a story that interests you, it can hardly be expected to keep a dinner companion alert.

Let's take a simple, brutal look at two pop-culture saints and icons of modern womanhood: the late, great Princess Di and her co-demiser, Mother Teresa. Diana played the starring role in a world-class drama of self-involvement. Her search for the right man, the right personality, the right shade of blonde, the right dress size, and, then, the right dress—all central projects for the self-involved woman—was enacted on the largest stage possible. Her quest for these key accessories of personhood obsessed the entire world. Mother Teresa, on the other hand, wore the same outfit every day. She was noted not for her focus on self, but for her focus on others. And though the latter quality may win more points on Judgment Day, there's no doubt whose funeral got better TV coverage. So I ask you: Which one would you have rather met for lunch?

SELF-JUDGING

Supreme Court Justice Ruth Bader Ginsburg

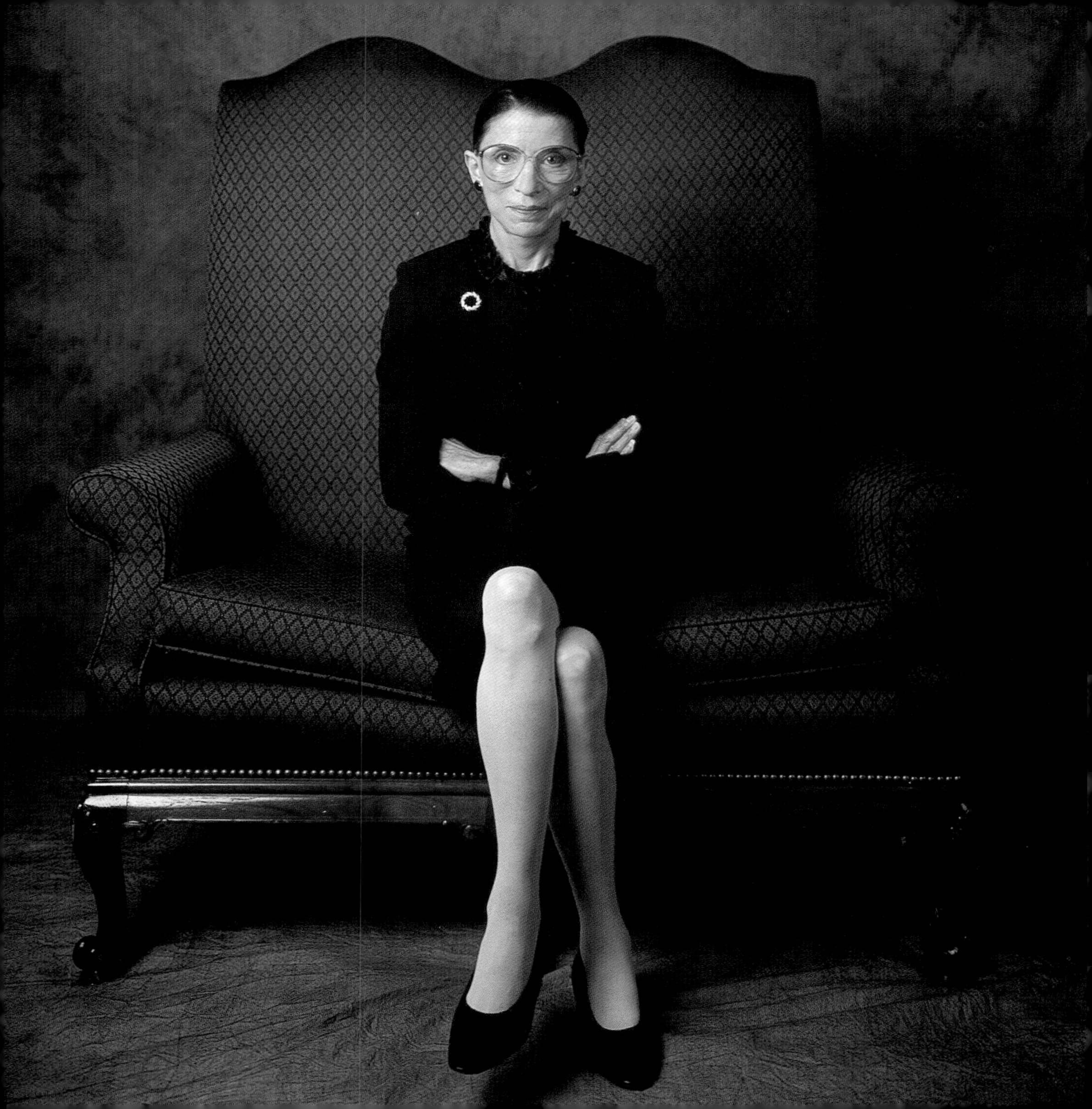

Self-Kn

by David Ansen

Criticism is a word with blood on its teeth—because we know

that another definition of criticism is "the act of finding

fault." Criticism's unsavoriness was drummed into us by our

parents: "If you can't say anything nice about someone,

don't say anything at all." But who listened? A person who

doesn't have anything bad to say about someone—or about a

owledge

work of art—may be a saint, but he's more likely a bore. We define ourselves, in part, by the discriminations we make. The value of what we love is enriched by our understanding of what we dislike. I criticize because I believe that splitting the fine hairs of art takes us deeper into ourselves and helps us to see both the work and the world with clearer eyes.

"Knowing
wisdom. Know
self is

others is
ing your-
enlightenment."

–Lao-Tzu

A CURE FOR SELF-LOATHING

by Alice Hoffman

The remedy, to be followed exactly—more or less:

Do not look in the mirror for three days and do not speak with anyone you suspect of agreeing with your current opinion of yourself.

On the first day: Wear blue; buy roses; fix something broken; polish furniture. Allow yourself a mistake; drink a mixture of lemon juice and water; cry all night, then go shopping for new pillowcases.

On the second day: Make jam; visit an acquaintance unable to leave the house due to illness, sorrow, or advancing years; fix a pot of tomato-rice soup and let simmer. Give your coats away to those who cannot stay warm. Forget what you couldn't or didn't do right. Run for two miles, paying attention only to the shape of leaves, the sound of birds, the idea of desire.

On the third day: Paint your bedroom; absolve an old enemy; braid your hair, or cut it all off. Think about November; imagine stars and clear skies; believe in possibilities and in hardship. Study signs; be grateful; consider devotion, moonlight, and your own dreams. Early in the morning, at the hour when the grass is damp and the sky above you is cracking open like an egg, walk a dog through your neighborhood. Then and there, while most people are still asleep in their beds, forgive yourself.

Self-Love

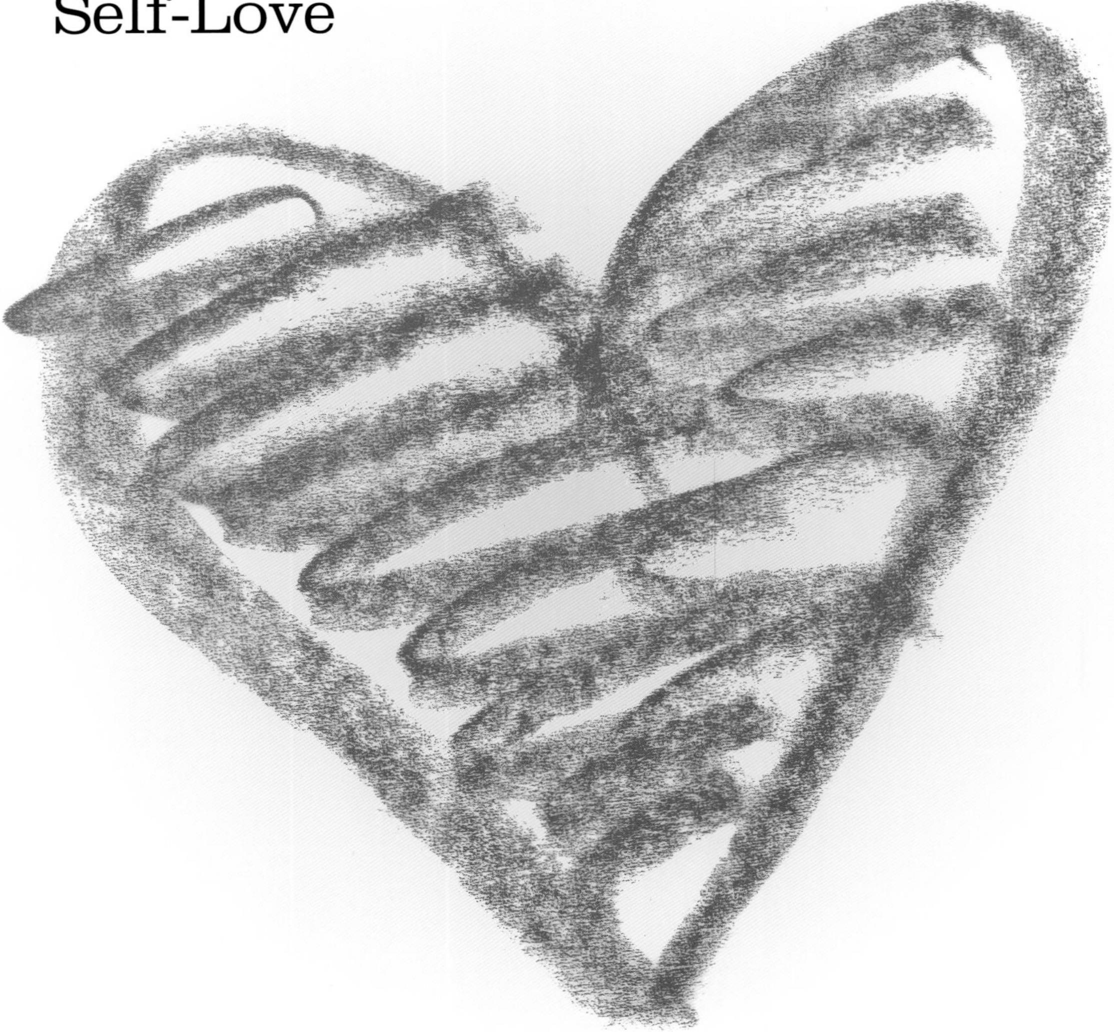

"*You really have to love yourself to get anything done in this world.*"

—LUCILLE BALL

Self-Love

by Lucy Grealy

"No one will love you unless you love yourself." The ultimate catch-22 in romance; right up there with "You'll find someone when you stop looking for someone." Throughout most of my twenties, I felt like a kid playing peekaboo; hey guys, look at me not looking. I mean, how was I supposed to know I was lovable, that I could love myself, unless someone loved me? On bad days, I'd feel forlorn and frustrated. On better days, I might be objective and curious enough to feel as if someone had just handed me a koan, a paradoxical question Buddhist monks give their disciples to meditate upon. What is the sound of one hand clapping? How do you love yourself?

At the end of my twenties, I lived on Cape Cod one winter, at the very lonely, isolated tip of a town that all the tourists abandoned for five months of the year. One restaurant and one bar stayed open; the rest of the town was shuttered up and a strong wind off the ocean water swirled the sand and snow together on the sidewalks. Of course, in this almost deserted town, I managed to find one person to fall in love with and, "of course" (as I saw it), he did not love me. It was one of the hardest times of my life, a time you could not pay me to live through again. And yet, clichéd as this may sound, one extraordinary thing did come out of it. Let me tell you about it. Not because it will happen this way for you, not because I'm going to reveal a secret, tell you the night-school course you can take, the book you can read, the skin-care product you can buy, the perfect black dress to wear— but because it's the way it happened.

This particular winter, there was a lot of weather. My top-floor apartment was in a wooden house just off the bay, and the wind was so strong some nights the entire apartment swayed very gently. The water in the toilet bowl slowly sloshed back and forth, as did the water in the bath if I filled it. I did fill it almost every night, because lying in the warm water, listening to the wind lament while it almost subtly rocked me was the only thing that soothed me.

I have this habit of buying and using a new bottle of shampoo before the old bottle is completely empty. As a result, I end up with about ten bottles of shampoo lining the edge of my bathtub, each with one inch of viscous goop at the bottom. One night I was lying in the bathtub, looking at the rows of near-derelict shampoo bottles, thinking my usual self-deprecating thoughts, employing the shampoo bottles as my straight men. "You big loser," I told myself. "Look at this pathetic collection; you can't even buy shampoo right."

Then I thought of Michael. This wasn't odd; all I ever did was think about Michael, about how wonderful he was, and how pathetic I was because he didn't love me. And then I looked at the shampoo bottles and thought of Michael's bathroom, which was a chaotic disaster. He didn't even use shampoo; he just washed his hair with bar soap. I found this utterly charming. Everything he did was utterly charming to me. Suddenly, I realized that if Michael had a collection of almost empty shampoo bottles lining his bathtub, that, too, would be charming. It would indicate to me how eccentric he was, how funny, how lovable. That last word hit me so hard, I half expected the water to fly out of the bathtub. It was lovable.

For the first time, I fully understood that I had an infinite capacity for love, and the fact that I'd never recognized this before was due to an almost laughable glitch, a simple misdirection. I was looking the wrong way: I thought the love had to come in. Yet now I saw that the answer was not in getting someone else to love me, but in recognizing that I was capable of loving someone else, of giving love out. If I could love another (and even if he didn't return it), then I could turn that love toward myself. It's slightly embarrassing to report that the first moment I was objectively able to view myself as a lovable person came about at that moment, in the bathtub, during that otherwise cold and lonely winter, but it's true. I was different forever—because of a row of shampoo bottles.

SeLf-MaDe

by Connie Porter

Last spring I attended the fifth-grade promotion at a school where I volunteer. The day before, I spent the afternoon with the third of the class that failed, including the student I tutored.

At lunch, those being promoted were practicing for the ceremony. Repeatedly they marched in the door of the cafeteria and to the stage in front. From the smallest to the tallest, they tried to master the simple step-to-gether-step-together rhythm that will take them down many aisles in life. Their line was ragged, their timing off, and when they sang, their voices were thinned, weakened by all those who were missing, those sitting with me, bitterly complaining about how stupid their classmates looked, how bad they sounded. I told them those things weren't true, and though it was hard to be happy for the others, they had earned the right to move on to middle school. A tall, quiet boy, Jamal, was the only one who said he would attend the promotion. "They my friends. I'm going to be taking that walk next year and I want someone to be there clapping for me," he explained. Jamal did attend the next day, clapping loudly as his classmates surprisingly marched in rhythm and in a neat, well-spaced line. When the assistant superintendent delivered his address, I was soberly reminded why so many students hadn't passed. He told those being promoted, "You are responsible for you being here today. No one else."

Before I started volunteering at the school, I was told that three-quarters of the children were from single-parent homes and nearly half had drug-addicted or alcoholic parents. I had chosen the school because it was so much like the elementary school I'd attended, drawing its students from public housing. It was only when the speaker pointed out that some of those children were self-made that I even thought about it.

Few of us think of the self-made woman we see at 30, polished and successful, as a self-made child at 10. Instead we marvel at what she has accomplished. Seldom do we think that for every one of her we see, there are many more we never meet.

The next time we hear about a self-made woman, I hope we do marvel. And that we realize that so many of her childhood moments of private sorrow and public joy were never shared with anyone. Not a boy like Jamal. Kind, and caring, and quiet, but watching every step.

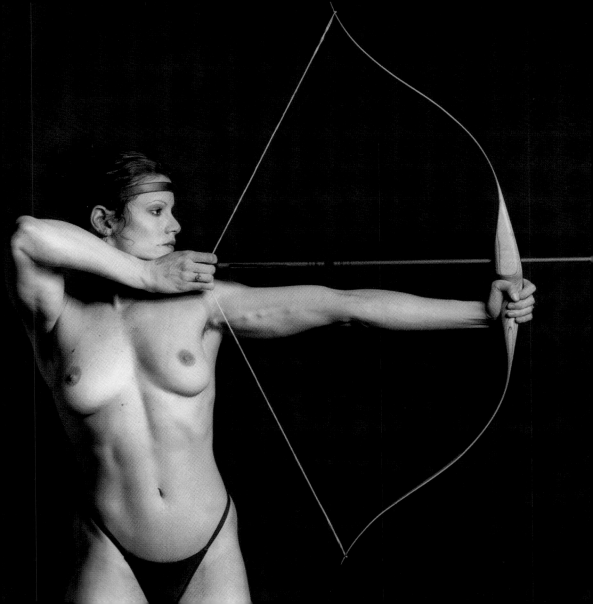

Self-Mastery

Robert Mapplethorpe
Lisa Lyons, 1982

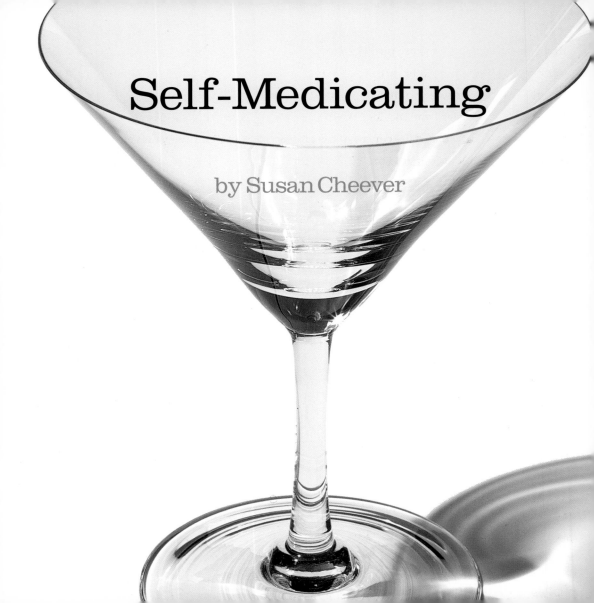

Self-Medicating

by Susan Cheever

All the time that I was growing up, drinking seemed as much a part of life—as ordinary a part of life—as eating, or even breathing. No one talked about it. There were plenty of signs, though. Guests were always falling down the stairs or trying—unsuccessfully—to vault over the furniture or swing from the door frames. People who came for Sunday lunch frequently had to be put to bed during the course of the afternoon. Sometimes they stayed for days. My mother brought them soup and did their laundry. The family cars made lots of trips to the body shop. In the evenings there were terrible fights. Of course I knew about alcoholics: They were old men in trench coats who had lost everything and disgraced their families, or they were housewives who nipped at the sherry and were passed out on the kitchen floor when their children came home from school. It never occurred to me that there was any connection between the problems we had as a family and the way we drank.

I've grown up a lot since then—and so has alcoholism. It's no longer acceptable to get falling-down drunk, or make passes at the wrong wife, or swing from the chandelier, or drink and drive. Martinis are for special occasions, many people have switched to drinking "just a little" white wine. But alcohol is doing as much harm as ever. It may look innocent, but it still kills. Forty percent of traffic fatalities are alcohol-related, twenty-five percent of hospital admissions are alcohol related, fetal alcohol syndrome is the leading case of mental retardation. More than thirty percent of high school seniors say they have been drunk in the past month. The unspeakable emotional damage done by alcoholism in families is beyond any statistics.

Has anything really changed? All of our knowledge of alcoholism and of recovery programs seems to have little effect on the statistics and no effect on the emotional injury rate. When we were children, alcoholism was acceptable. These days it's hidden . . . in plain sight. It's time to look at what's right there in front of us. It's time to grow the rest of the way up.

Self-Perp

I know all the right reasons for wanting a child: because you love to nurture; because you adore small beings; because, as a girl, you fussed over your dolls, powdering their tiny parts and loving the eerie eyes of these plastic people.

None of these reasons applies to me. I didn't play with dolls, and children, frankly, frighten me with their brute honesties, their rapturous hungers. And yet here I am, nearly seven weeks pregnant and planning on keeping it, if it will keep me. Why? I ask myself, and then I go back; I see myself as a very young girl in a home that was not right. I was four, I was five, and sad for so many reasons. Our kitchen tiles glittered in a winter way; the stove, shined to perfection, blurted back my face to me, and it was frightening how twisted and thin I looked. Always, in the morning, there was the sound of my mother crying in the kitchen; her sadness and rage made her impenetrable, and this was maybe my greatest loss. I grew up missing her, and thus, in so many ways missing myself. I can feel the space inside me still.

But now, inside me, slotted within that space, or in a sac of its own, a little being

AMY ECHE/STONE STONE IMAGES

etuating

by Lauren Slater

thrashes and grows. Yesterday, on the ultrasound screen, I saw the heart, and even though the image was grainy, all "black-and-white", I saw the baby's heart as scarlet; I picture the embryo itself as scarlet, as crimson, a Christmas ornament floating in my belly, giving off its own kind of glow. At night, I close my eyes and watch the glow, and then I watch the baby itself and I hate to say it—it's so narcissistic—but I see me in there, small and devolved, flesh to fur to frog to a brand-new set of cells, starting again, starting again. This is what I want: the chance to start my childhood over again. In having a child, in perpetuating myself, I am giving myself not only the chance to go forward, but maybe, more important, the chance to go back. If I am lucky enough to carry to term, this child will come into a home without winter glitter, impenetrable barriers, lovelessness. I will partake of the ancient parent's promise to make it right for her, for him, and thus, in some folded, backward way, for me as well. Self-perpetuation is just another form of self-revision, self-improvement, an opportunity to take back time.

SELF-PITY

by Patricia Marx

Poor me. Nobody loves me.

Actually, somebody might. But my phone machine is broken so I will never know. Let's just say I had no calls. That way, I can feel worse, which makes me feel better.

Just don't feel sorry for me. I can do that for myself. Besides, the prospect of someone feeling sorry for me is mortifying. It seems condescending, almost malicious.

Self-pity, on the other hand, comes out of pure kindness. It is a means of displaying self-love without appearing smug. It is martyrdom with the volume turned down inaudibly low. And there is so much to feel bad about! That you are 5'3" instead of 5'10". That no one left a message on your phone machine all day (or alternatively, that you have too many calls to return). That you didn't receive the National Book Award for poetry this year (even though you have never written a poem in your life). That the restaurant ran out of Dover sole just before you decided to order it. That you have a blister on your toe (surely, nobody has known suffering like you have!). That you have too many letters in your name, which makes it tedious to write your signature. That everyone else has a perfect life.

Self-pity is best experienced alone—in the bathtub, the car, the line at Motor Vehicles. It goes well with music (self-blues, preferably) and alcohol (anything but sangria). Unlike self-hatred, self-pity is a way of making yourself feel appreciated, spending quality time with someone you care about, allowing yourself to eat the whole bag of pretzels. If self-pity had a PR person, it would be renamed "self-compassion." Self-pity is always engaging—because it's so relevant. And rewarding. You didn't receive the birthday present you hoped for? Go out and buy it. They don't have the shoes you want in your size? Buy a dress you don't need. It rains during your vacation? Call the concierge and arrange for a massage. In the meantime, wallow in front of a pay-per-view movie on TV. If you are very good at self-pity, you will regard a story about famine, war, or terminal illness as feel-good entertainment compared to the tragedy of, say, having gained three pounds over the holidays.

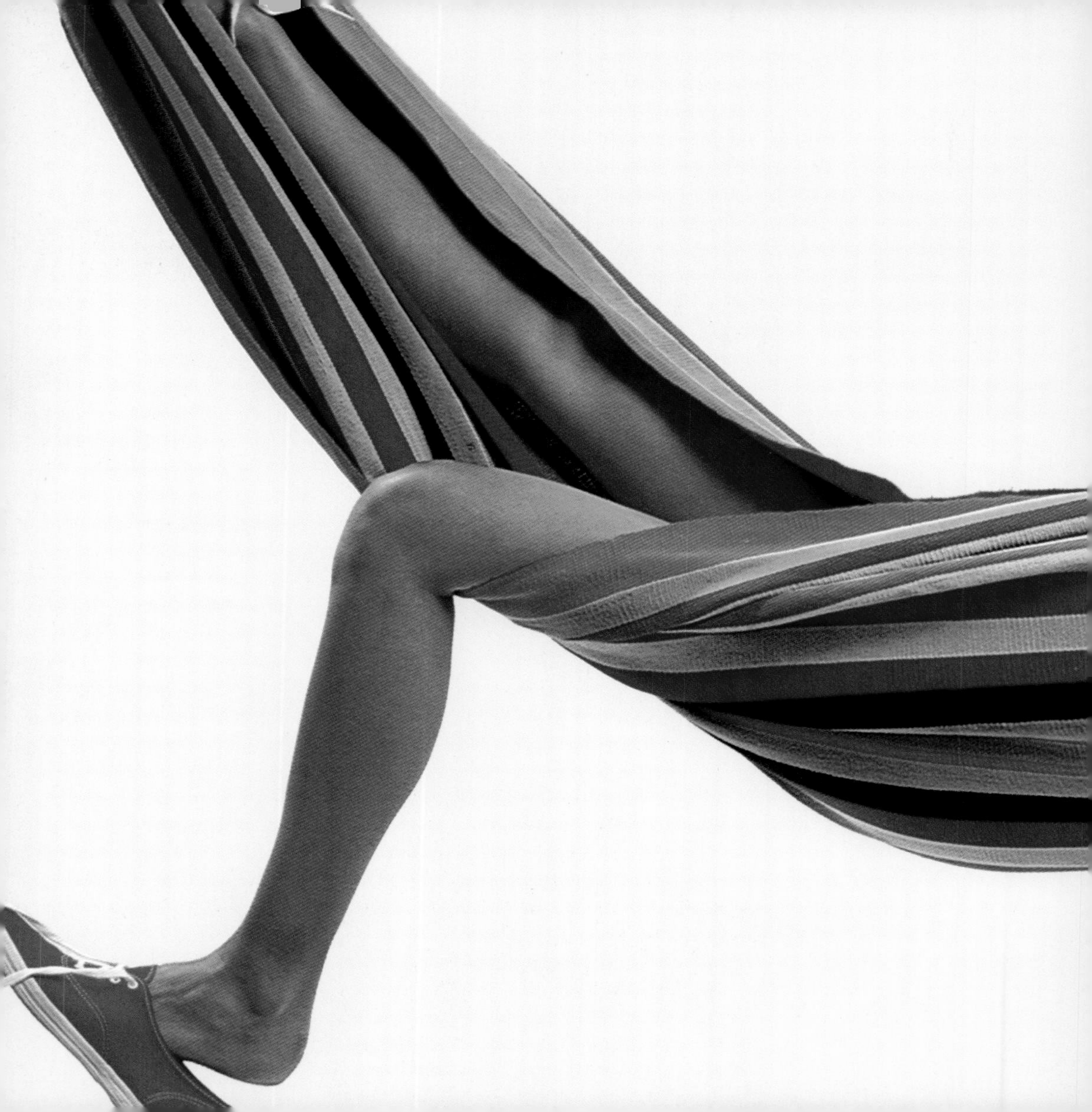

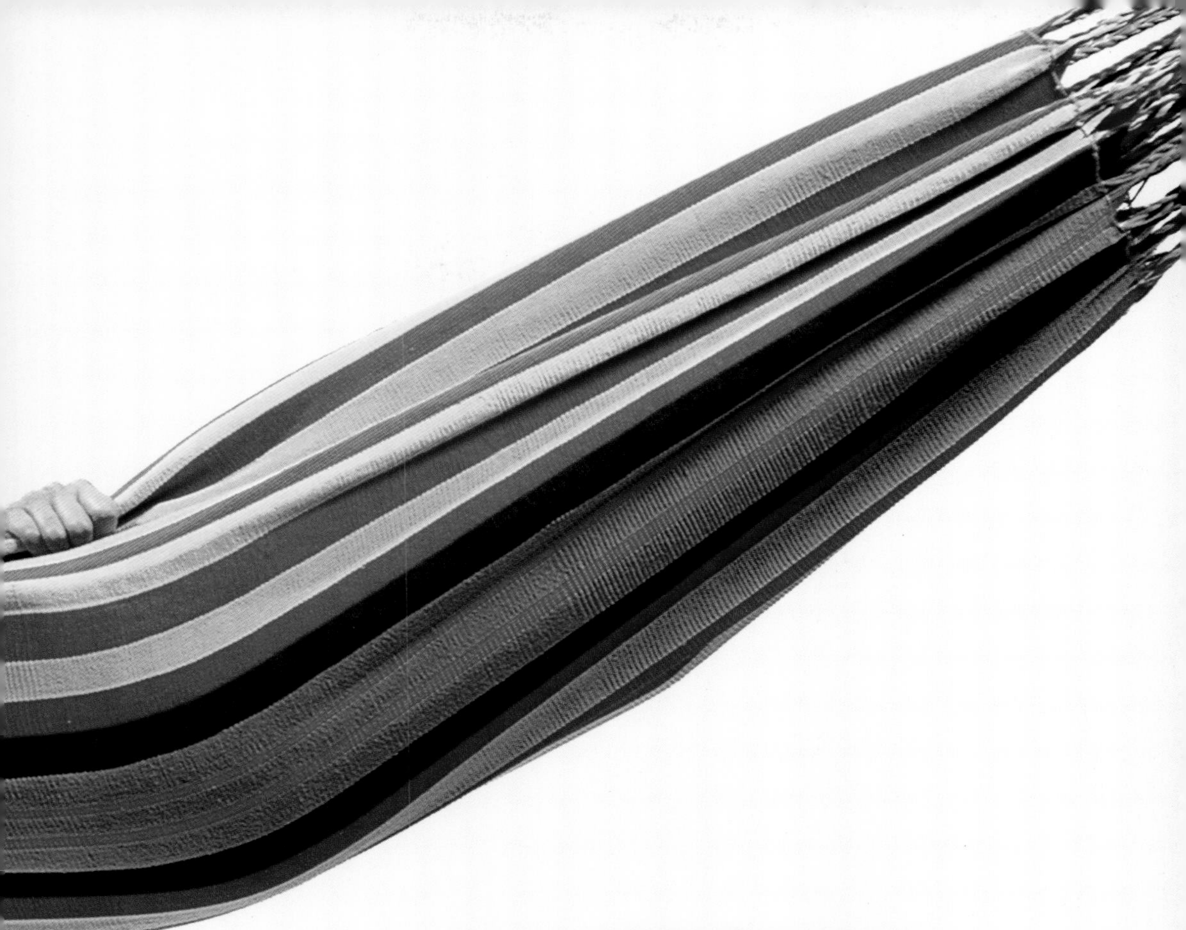

Self-Pleasing

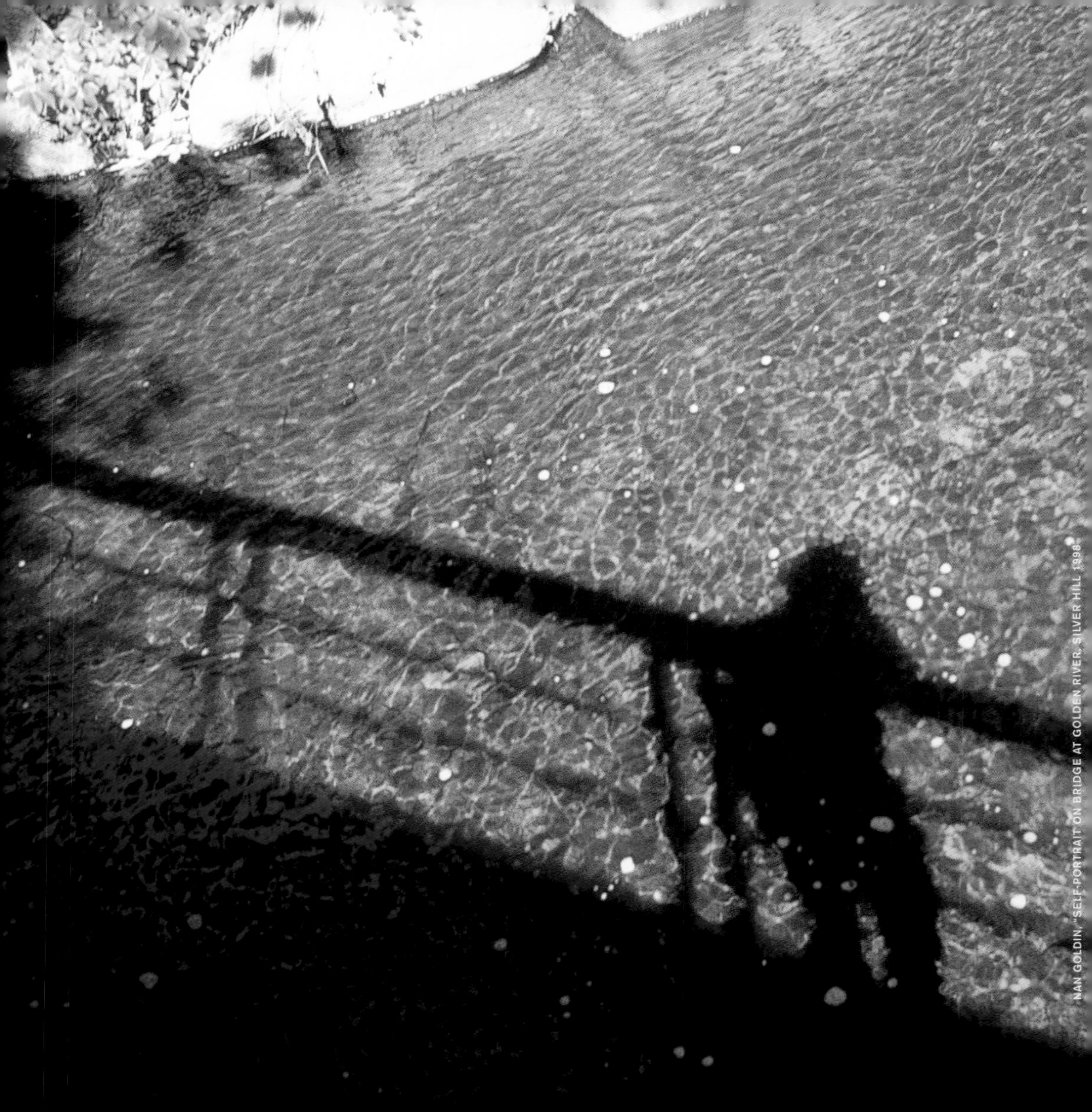

NAN GOLDIN, "SELF-PORTRAIT ON BRIDGE AT GOLDEN RIVER, SILVER HILL 1998"

SELF-PORTRAIT
Nan Goldin

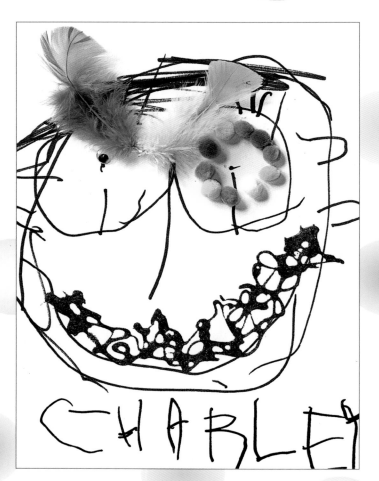

Self-Portrait

**Charley
Yoshimura,
age 5**

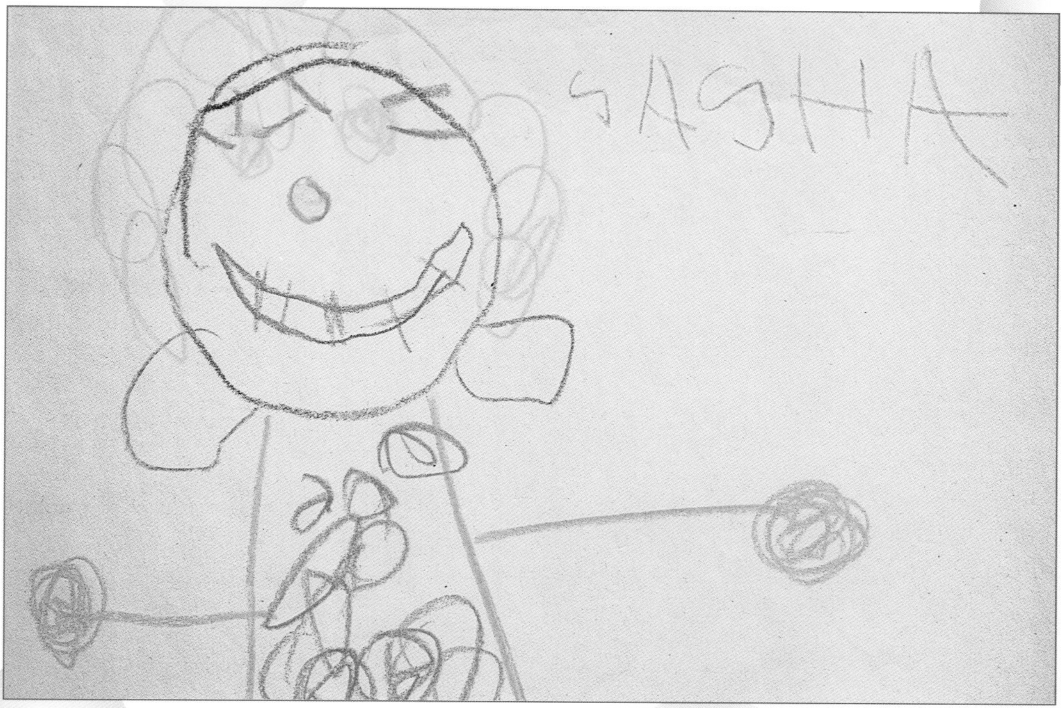
SASHA

Sasha Listfield Dudding, age 5

Self-Portrait

Self-Portrait
Annie Leibovitz

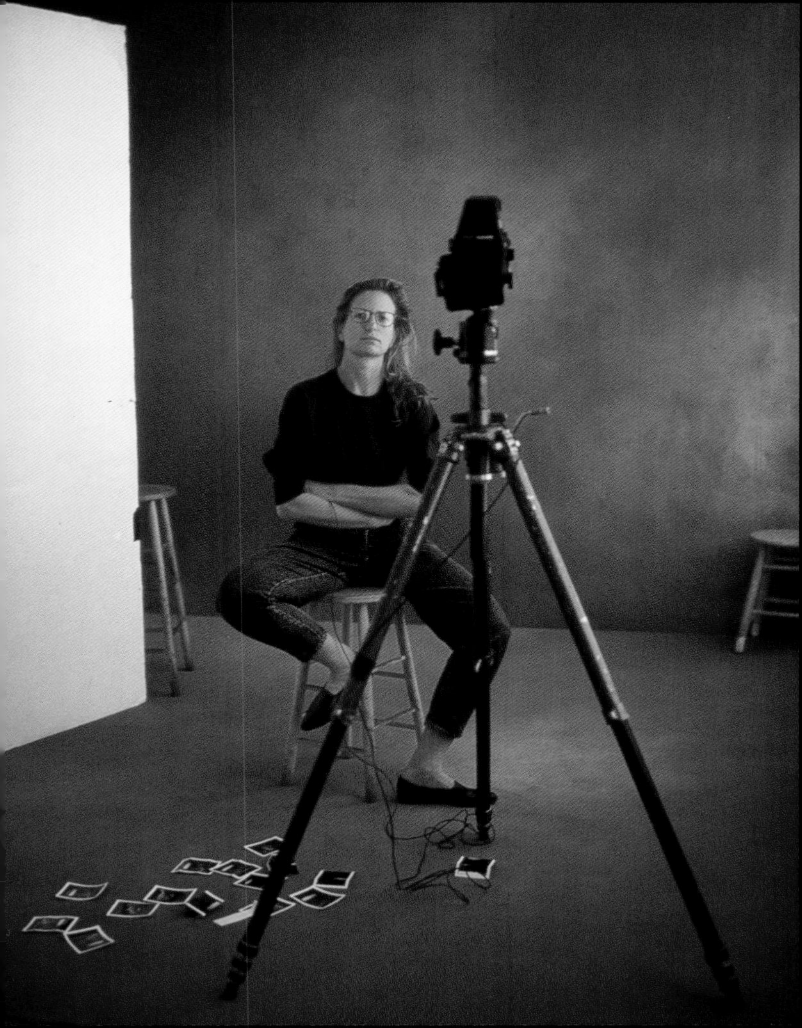

Self-Portrait

Jamie Lee Curtis

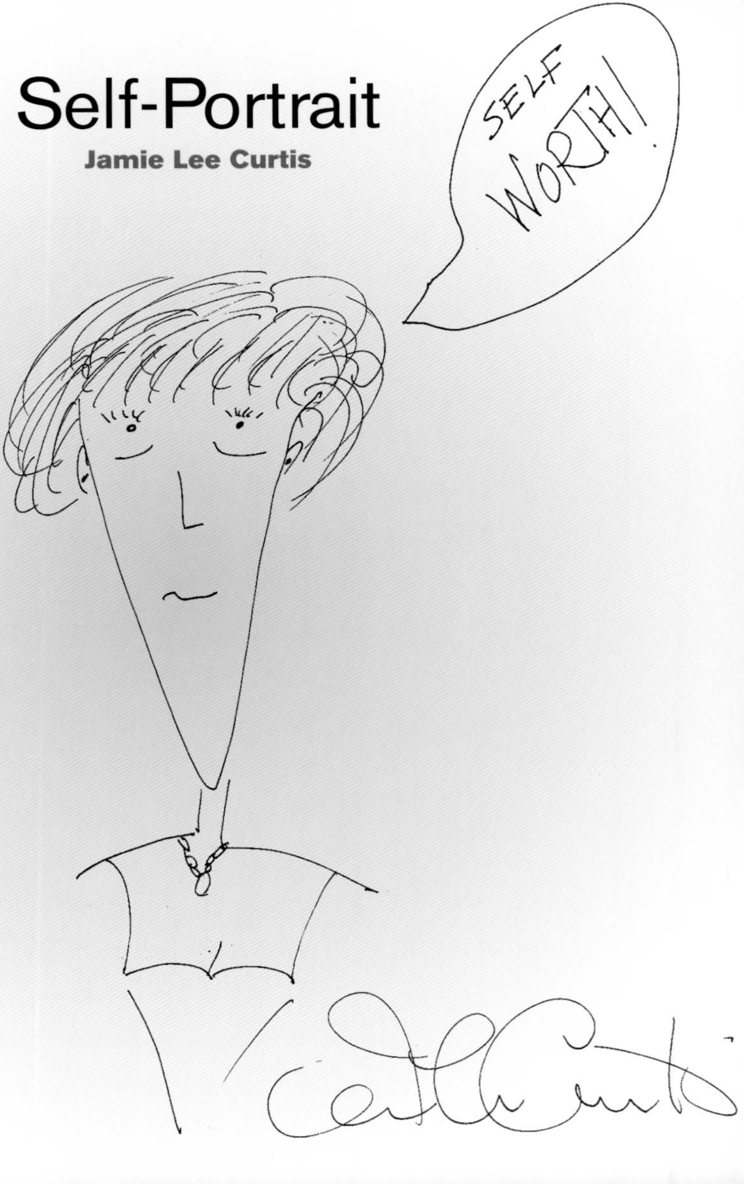
SELF WORTH!

Self-Portrait

Molly Shannon

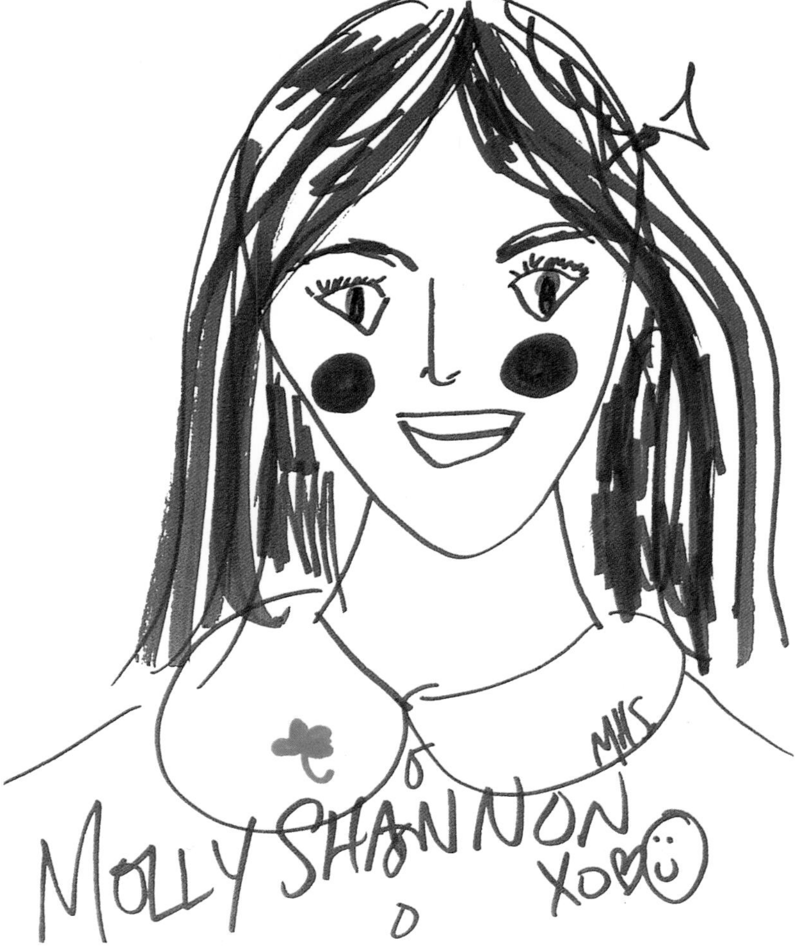
MHS
MOLLY SHANNON
XO

Self-Port

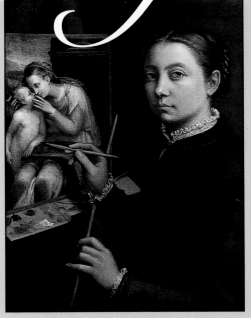

Sofonisba Anguissola (1535–1625)

Elizabeth Vigee-LeBrun (1755–1842)

raits

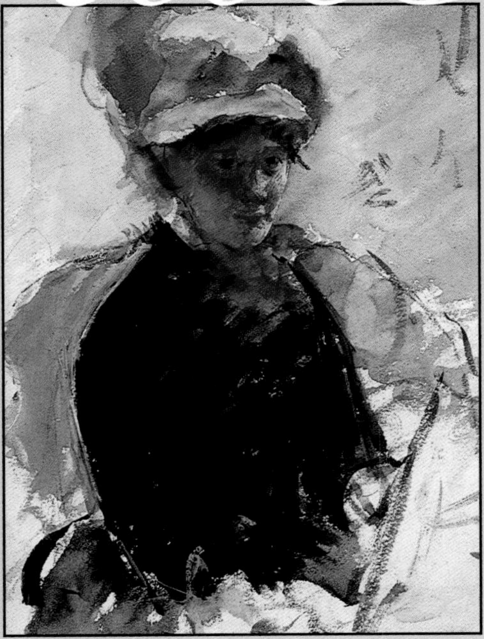

Mary Cassatt (1844–1926)

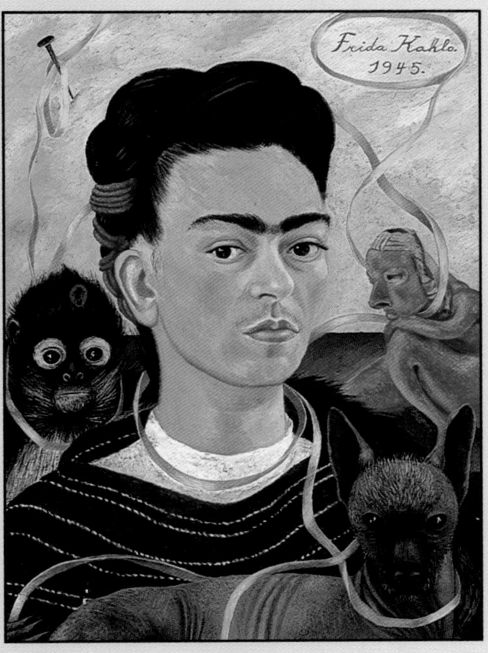
Frida Kahlo.
1945.

Frida Kahlo (1907–1954)

Self-Portraits

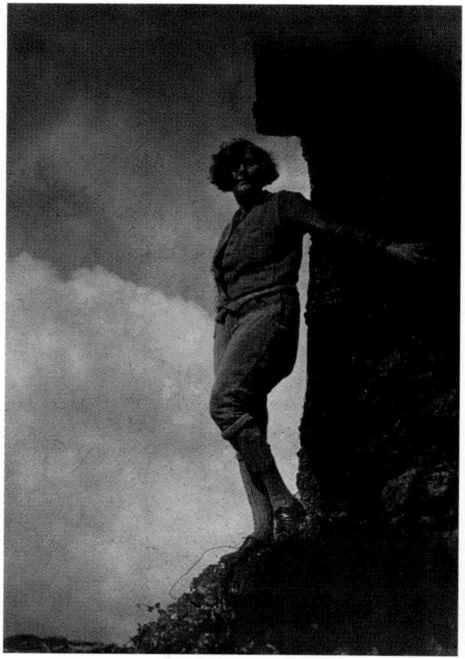

COURTESY GEORGE EASTMAN HOUSE

Anne Brigman, *Self-Portrait: Glory of the Open* 1920

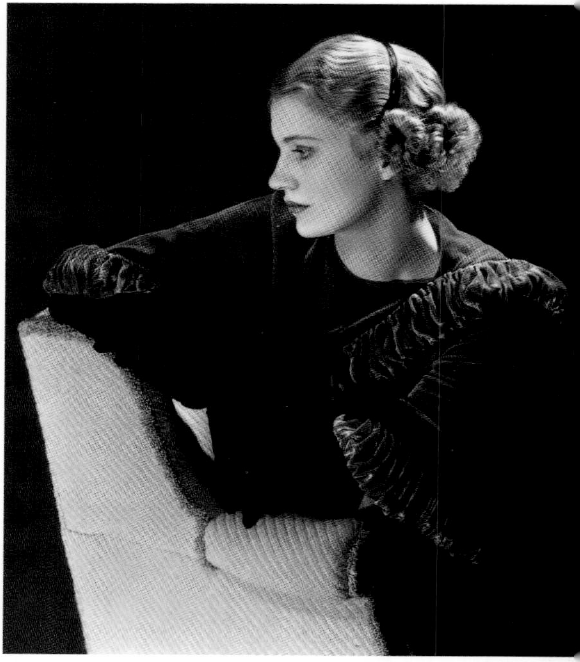

Lee Miller, *Self-Portrait, New York* 1932

Imogen Cunningham, *Self-Portrait* ca. 1906

Self-Possessed

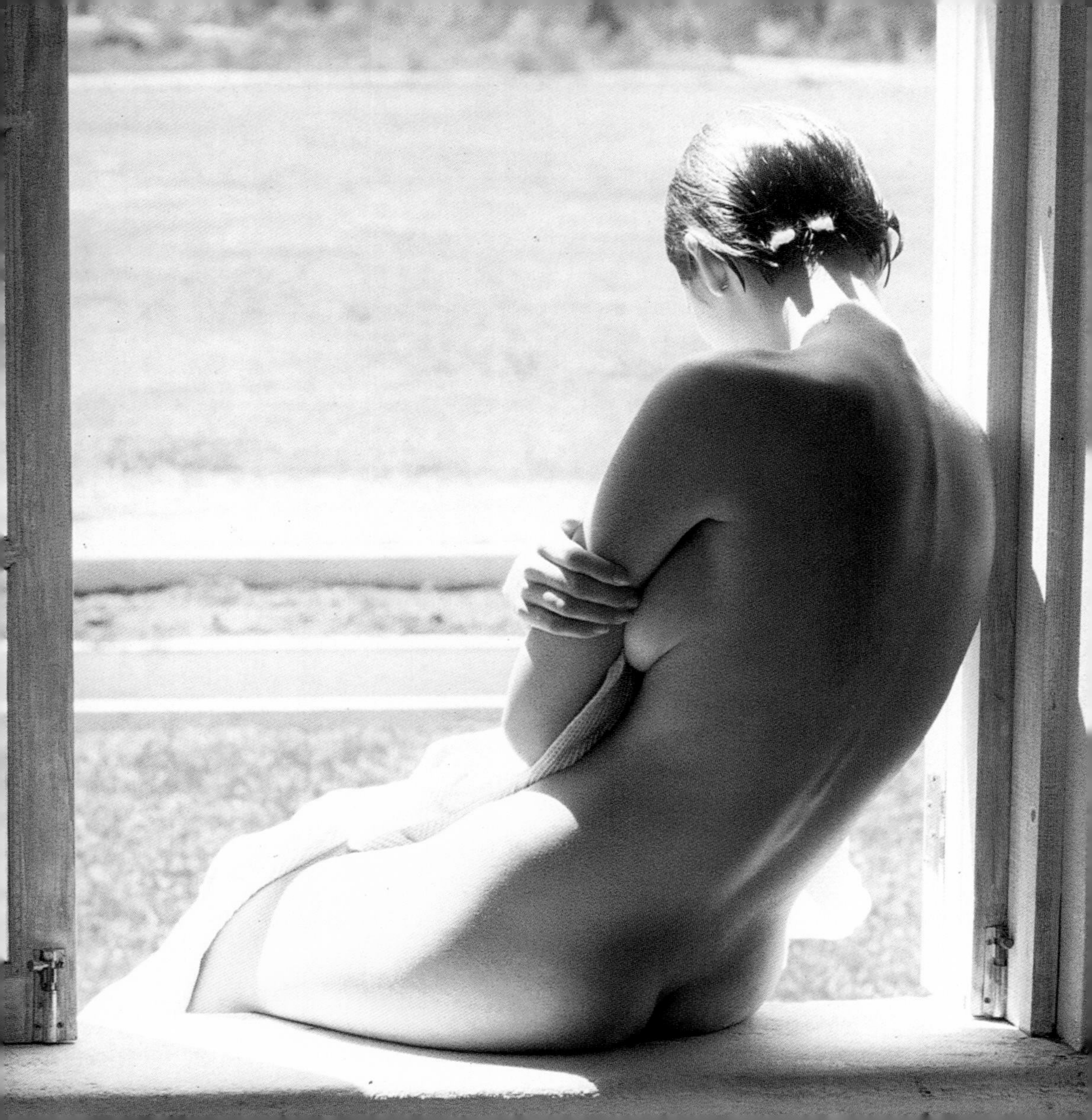

Self-Promotion

Self-Parody

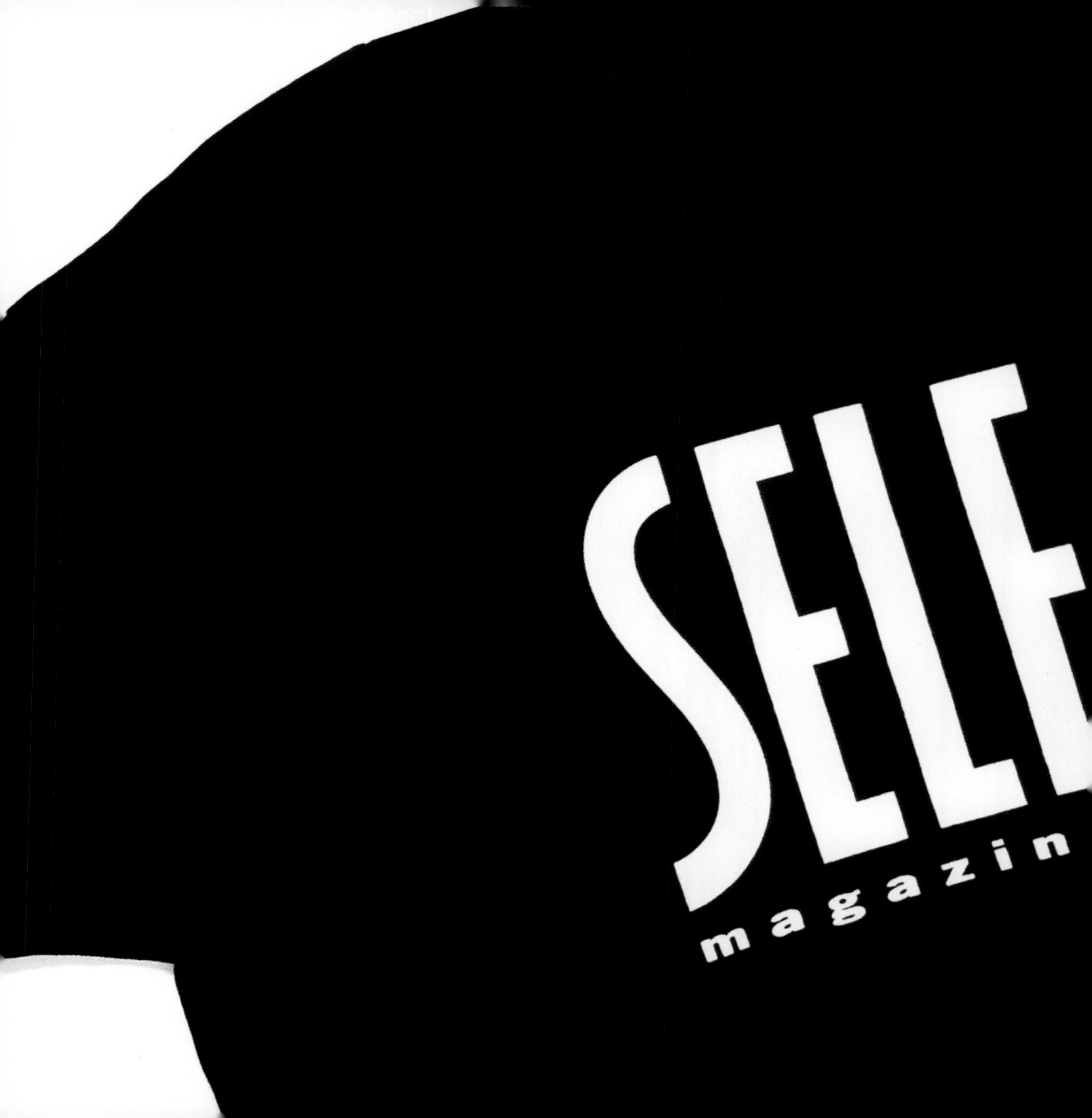
SEL
magazin

-Promotion

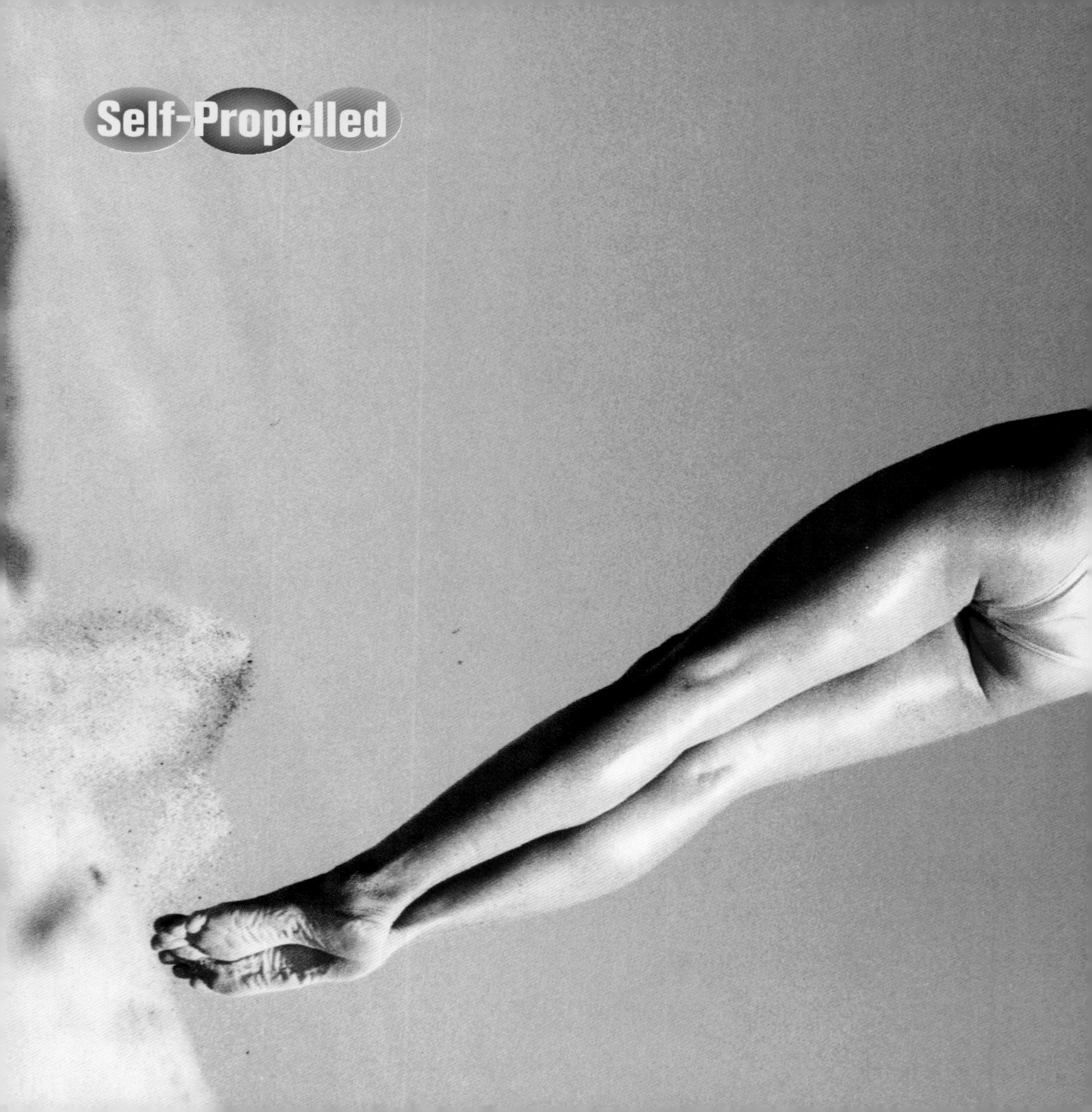
Self-Propelled

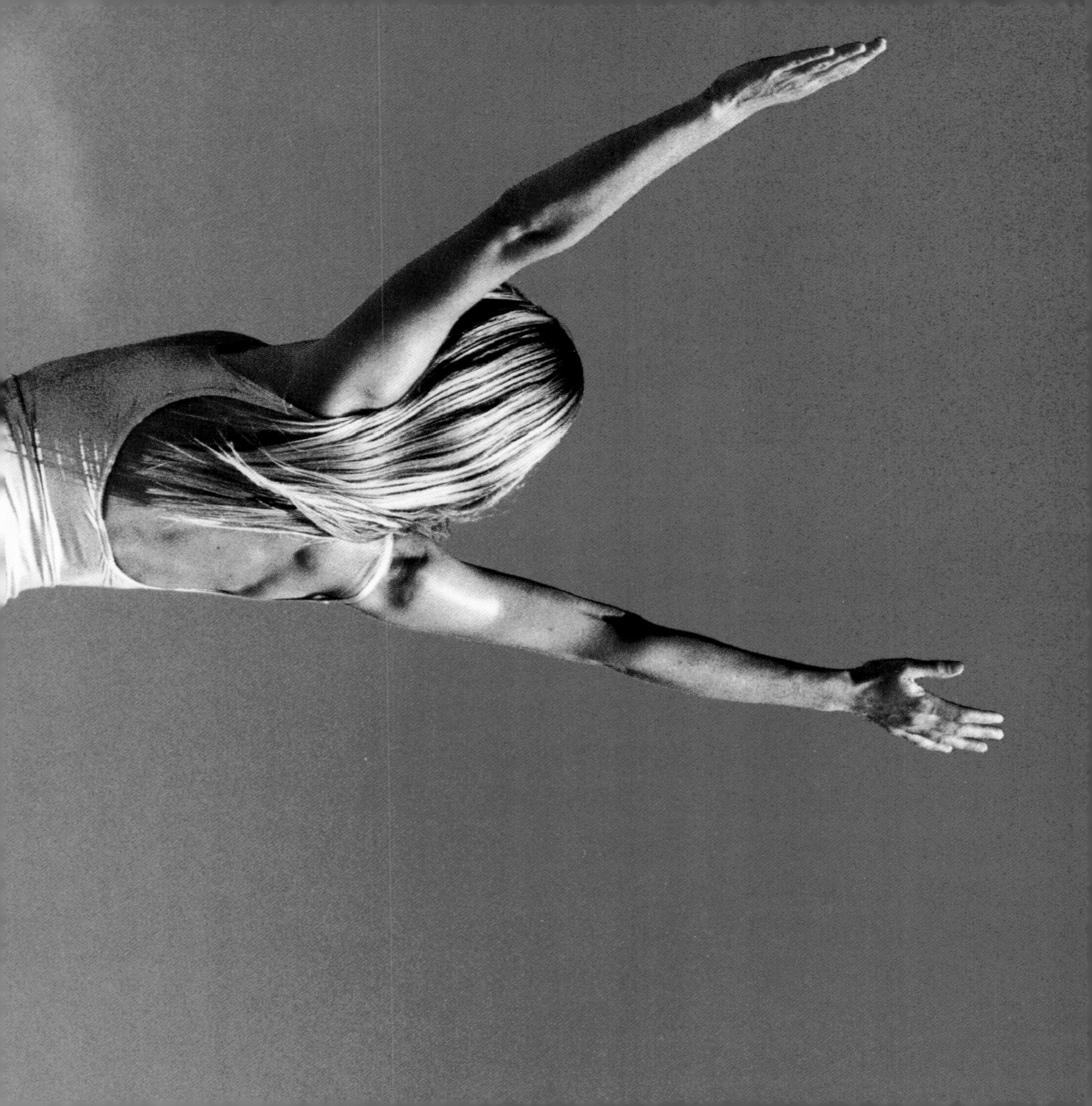

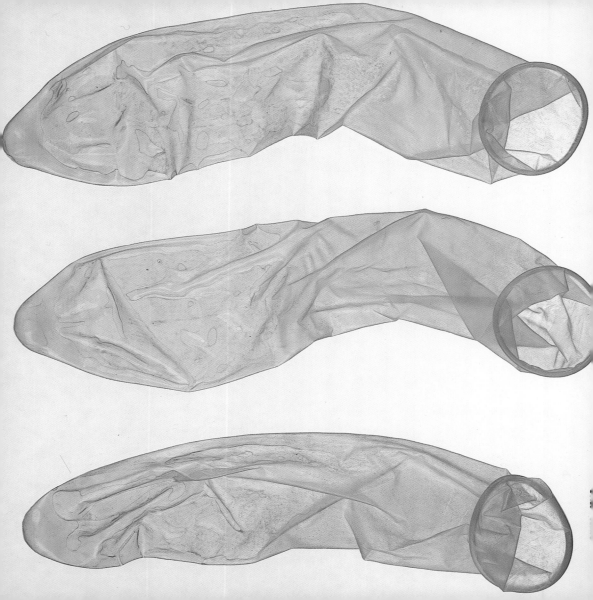

Self-Protection
by Karin Cook

My first job came completely naturally. An enthusiastic condom-user since college, I supported myself in graduate school trafficking in latex for $6.00 an hour. Working for the first chain of condom stores in the U.S. was an honor, so I traded health insurance and sick time for an inflated title and a chance to be part of something cutting edge and important. It wasn't retail, I told myself; it was more of a revolution. I quickly turned my enthusiasm into expertise, getting certified in health education and condom negotiation, and soon I spent my days talking to hundreds of customers about their fears, their relationships, and their sex lives. We had customers of every orientation, but not surprisingly, it was straight women who comprised the largest piece of the consumer pie. Full of questions and concerns about condoms, these women were educated, all right—chiefly in men's reluctance to wearing them. My suggestions of scented, contoured, ultrathin, plus-sized, and ribbed usually reminded them that it probably wasn't the condom that was the problem.

One day a regular customer came in to stock up on a supply of BeyondSevens, her favorite brand. While I was ringing up her wares, she played catch-up with a male coworker, informing him that she had moved, changed careers, learned to Rollerblade and gotten a new boyfriend. After she left, he turned to me and added thoughtfully, "Different guy, same condom." Condom negotiation is about compromise, not between people as much as between ideas. In the world of safer sex, one trades some spontaneity for security and some pleasure for protection. It's a trade worth making—an expression of loyalty to a self that needs protecting.

Self-Questioning

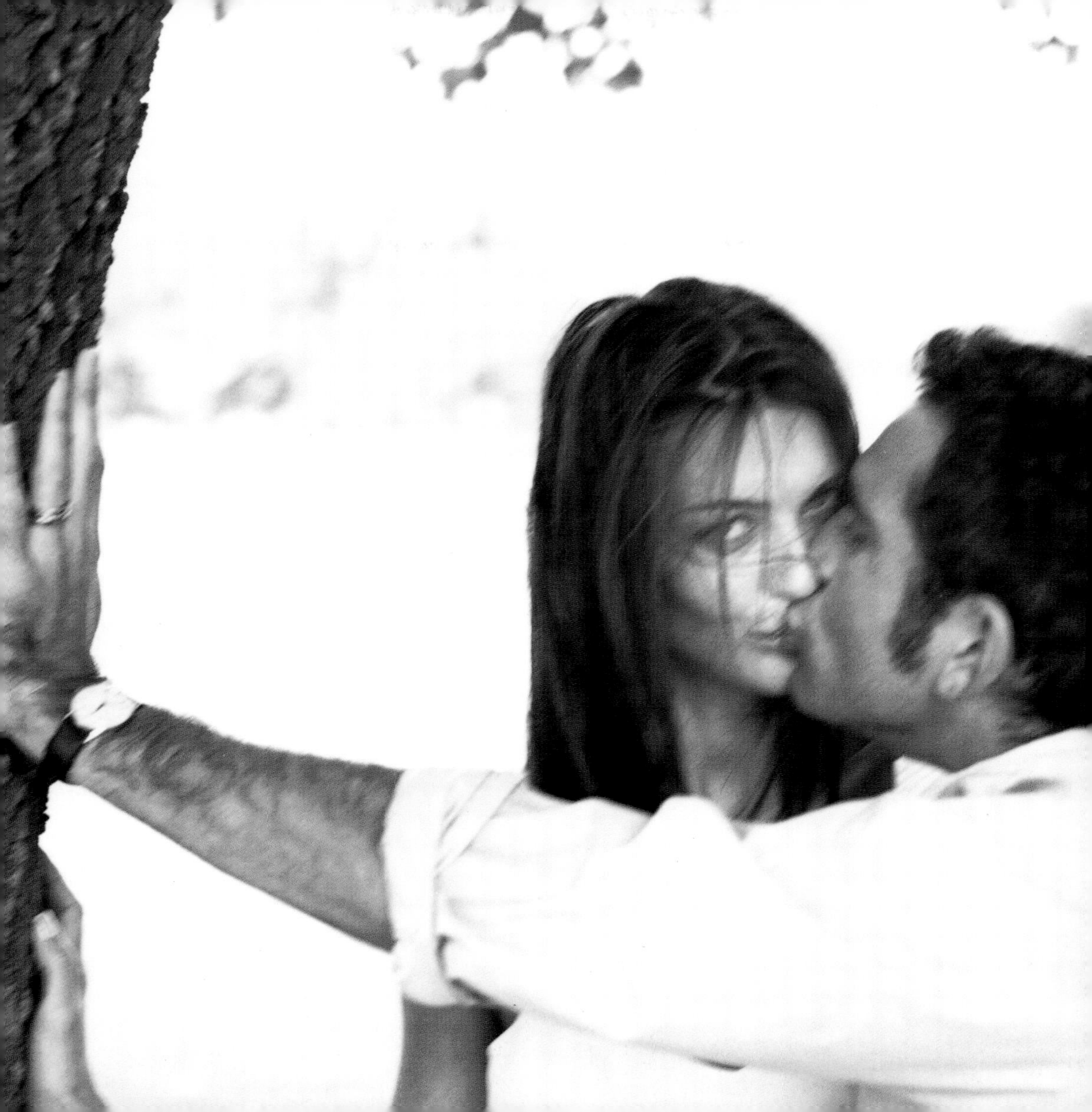

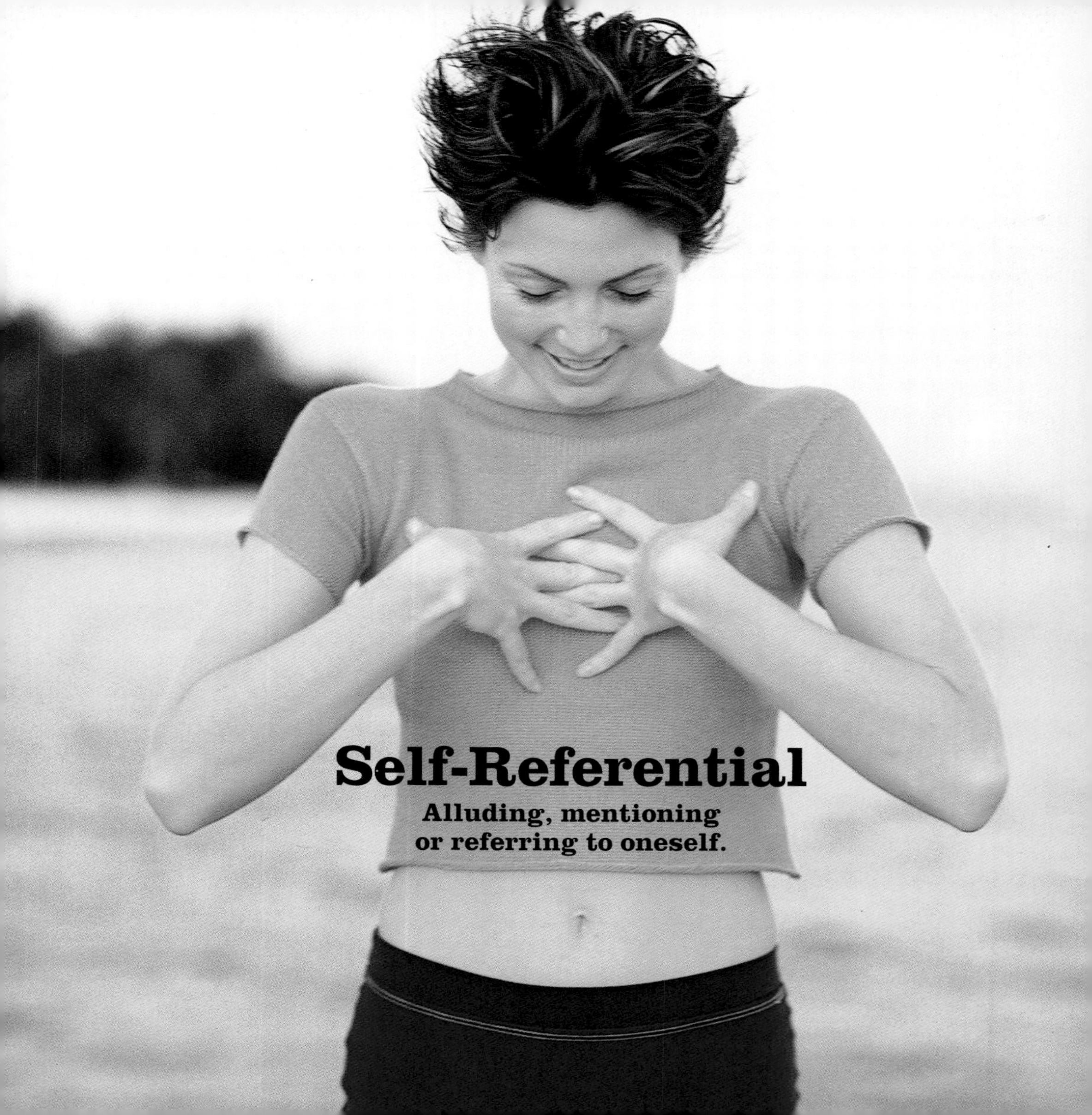
Self-Referential
Alluding, mentioning
or referring to oneself.

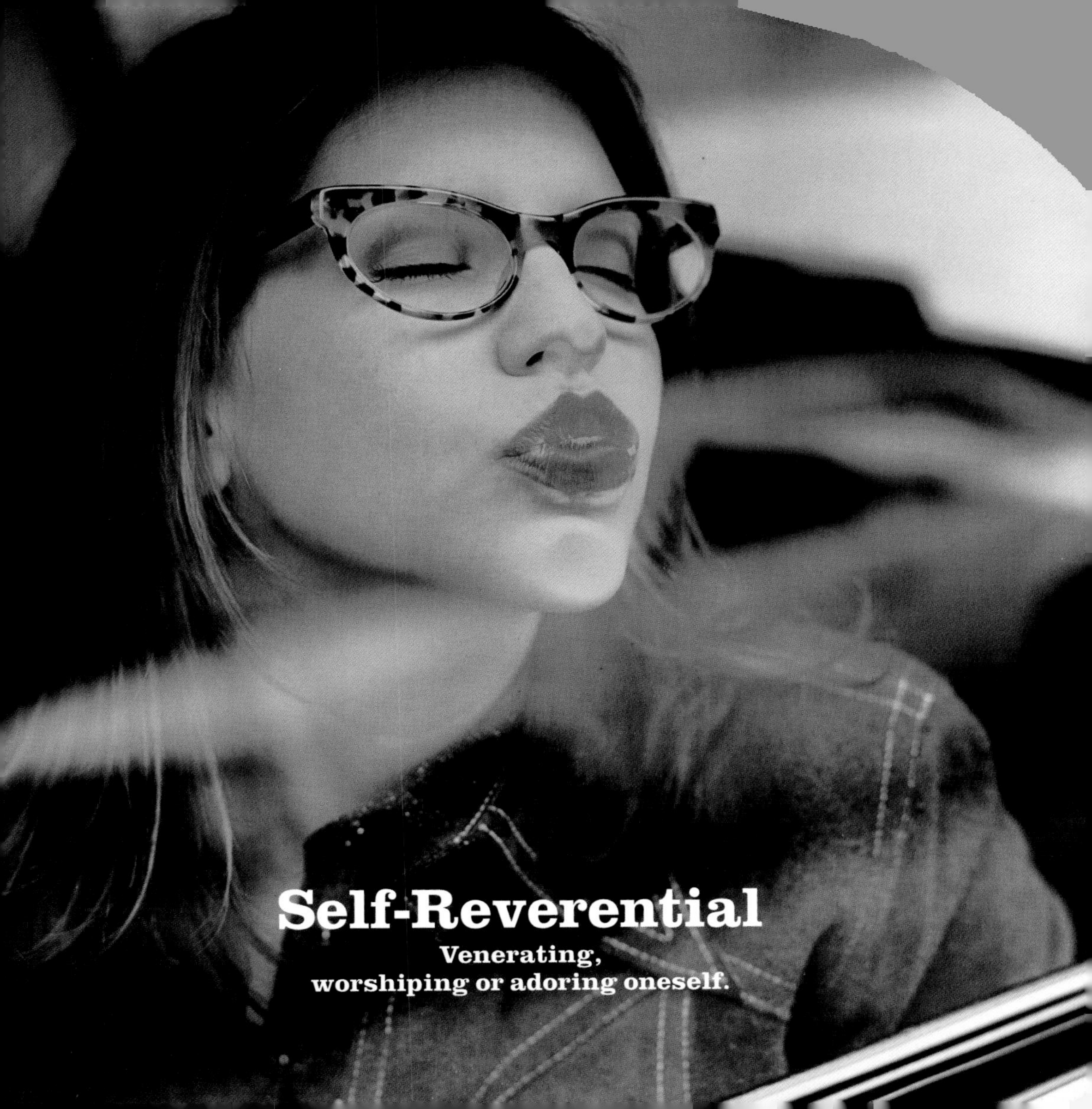
Self-Reverential
Venerating,
worshiping or adoring oneself.

Self-Reflective

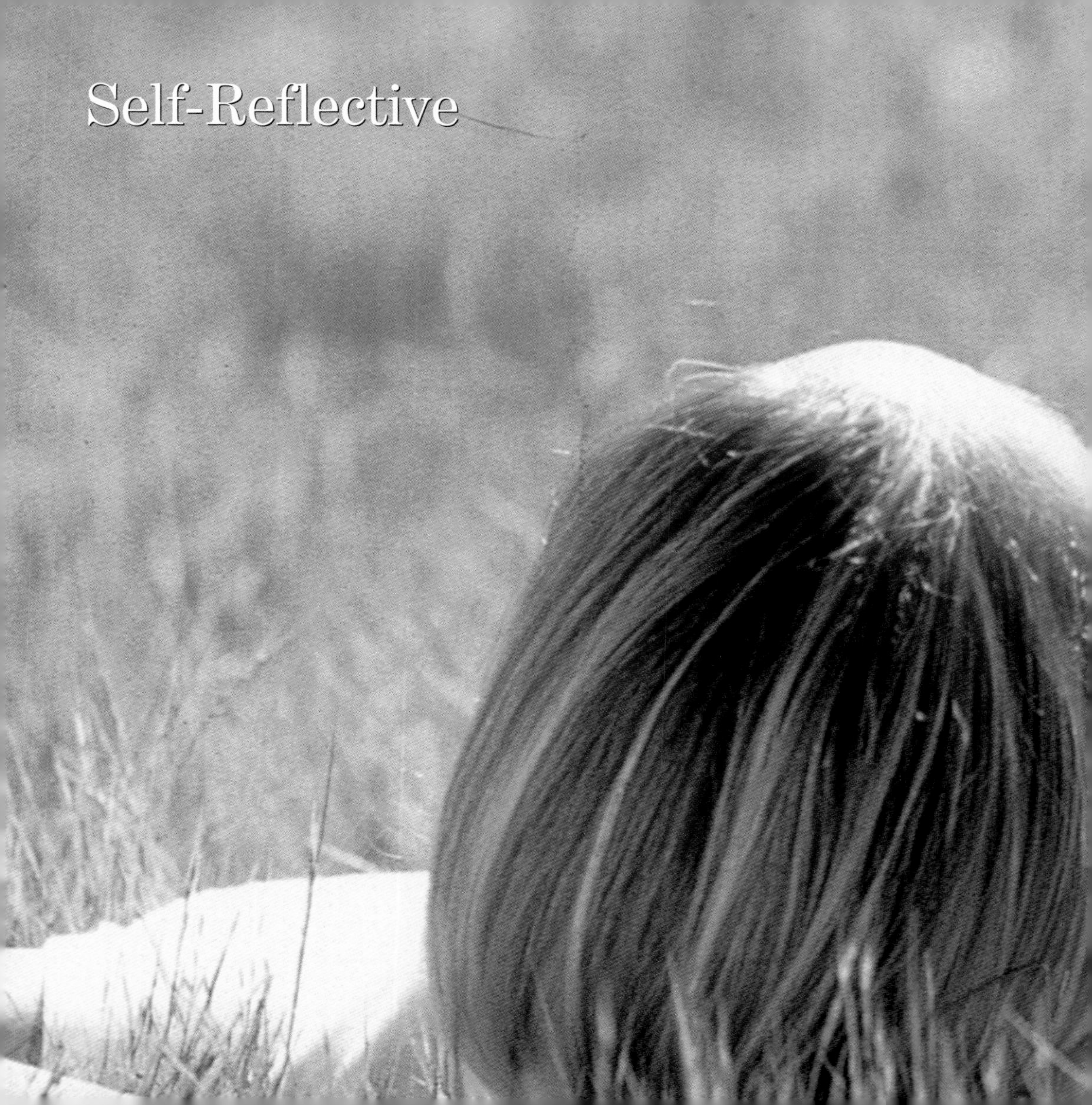

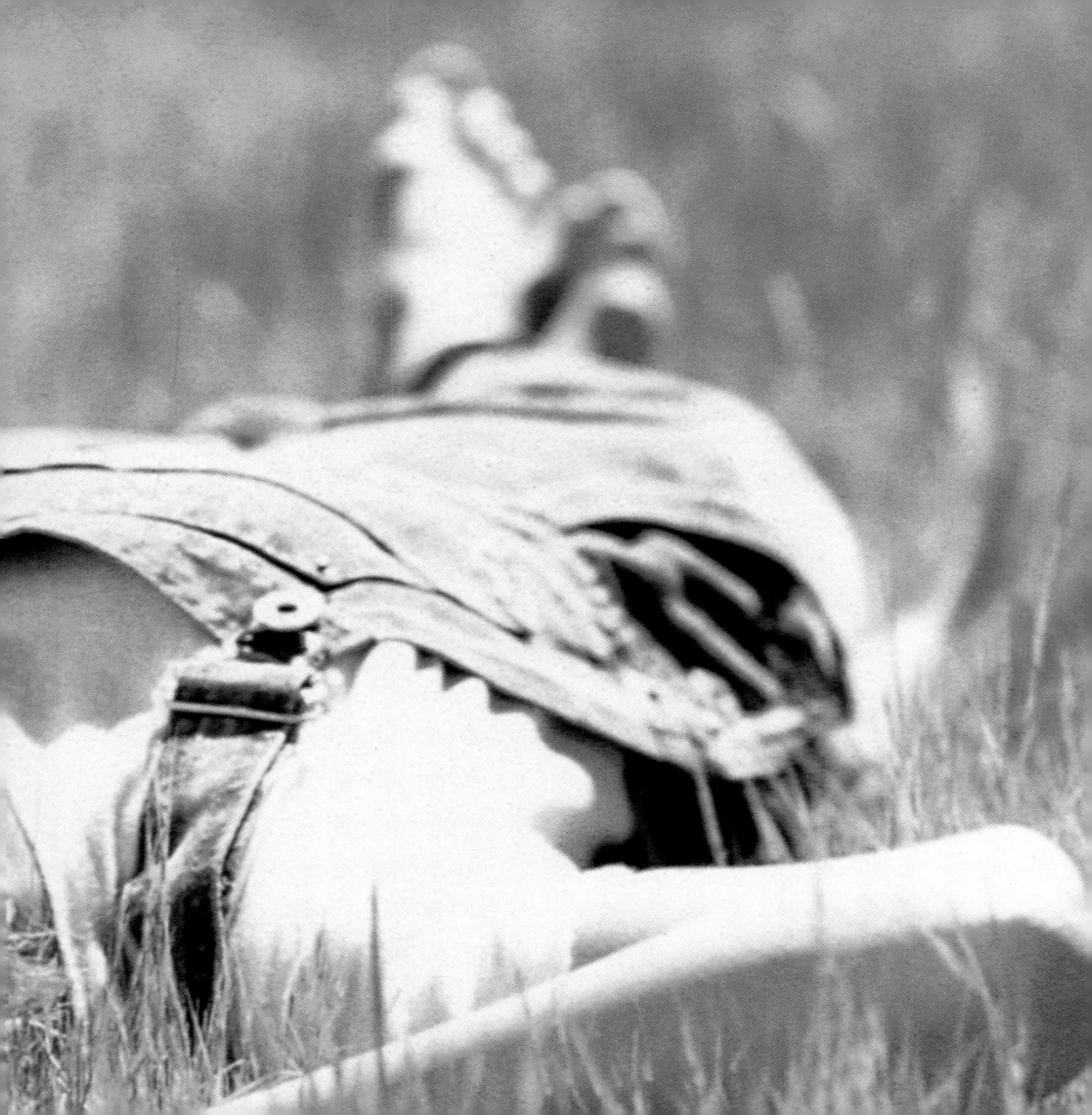

Rachel was dying. It seemed incongruous. Nobody died in Los Angeles, city of light, health, beauty. But it was true. She was dying The doctor gave her the diagnosis that morning. The disease had spread through her body, he said. It was too late for cures. She had four weeks, maybe five, to live. Light streamed in through the window behind the doctor, turning him into a silhouette. He was Jewish, handsome, and bearish, the type of man she was supposed to end up with in a perfect world. Funny. She was ending up with him all right. He would be the last man to touch her, the last man to lull her to sleep.

He wanted to know why she hadn't come to see him earlier. Perhaps they could have caught it. After all, she'd been suffering symptoms for over a year: dramatic weight loss, fever, low energy, nausea, diarrhea, fainting spells. Yet she had suffered in silence. She told the doctor she had stayed away because she was afraid to hear the truth.

She didn't tell him her real reason: She had not wanted the disease to end. She'd been praying for a new body for so long, that when she finally got it, she didn't dare ask questions. She had transformed into the woman she'd spent her whole life envying. Therapists had always told her weight loss wouldn't bring her happiness, that she had to look inside, but therapists were wrong. It had made her happy. A new body, she learned, could alter everything.

She was the proof. After four years of unwanted celibacy, a fellow actor—a man so beautiful she'd assumed he was gay—had asked her out on a date. Strangers on the street mistook her for someone famous. Her acting coach told her she had never looked better. She was getting callbacks to auditions.

by Danzy Senna

She no longer had to play the frump, the fat girl, the lump in the background. Even her skin seemed different. It had taken on a waxy, poreless shine, like the airbrushed faces she saw in fashion magazines.

What she'd suspected all her life was true: Thin girls really did live in an alternate universe, the world of the visible, the seen, the desired. It astounded her.

Now she walked out of the doctor's office into the glare of the parking lot. She slipped into her car, still secretly pleased by how little space she took up. She felt a little dizzy and gulped her bottle of water, before starting up the car. The parking attendant was a Mexican girl of maybe 18. She was pregnant and scooping bites of ice cream out of a dish. She put the dish down and clumsily got to her feet to ring up the bill. "One-seventy-five," she said.

Rachel blushed. That was how much she used to weigh. That was the number she had stared at each morning, the one she could never slip below—before the illness. She wondered for a brief moment if the pregnant girl was seeing the old Rachel, the fat girl, and she looked down at herself to check. But she was tiny. Her legs didn't meet in the middle, even sitting down. The doctor had just weighed her. She was in the double-digits. The pregnant girl cleared her throat. She was waiting, quietly, with her hand outstretched, to be paid, so she could get back to her ice cream.

Rachel placed the exact change in the girl's plump hand and thought the word *gordita* to herself with a slight, pleased giggle. As she moved forward, out of the lot, she imagined the ice cream expanding inside of the girl, ballooning into her hips and breasts and belly. Rachel, on the other hand, could eat all the ice cream she wanted. It would just pass right through her, like water, leaving no trace behind.

171

Self-Reliance

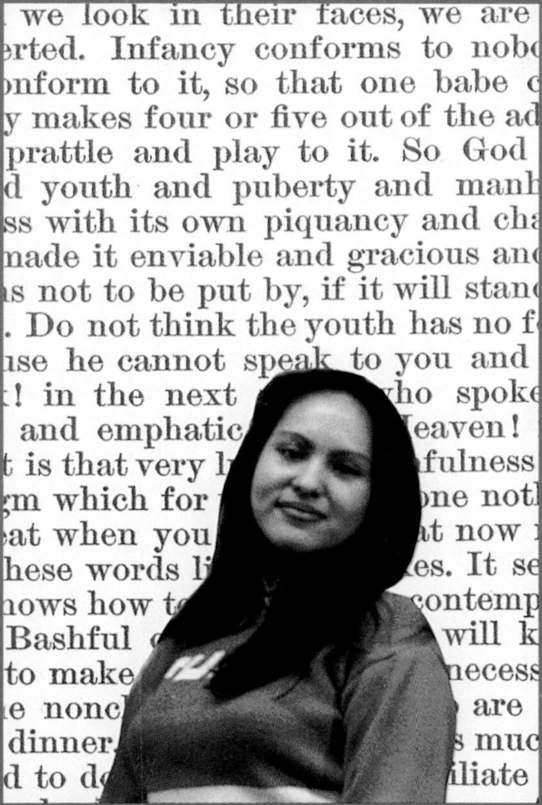

we look in their faces, we are
erted. Infancy conforms to nobo
onform to it, so that one babe
y makes four or five out of the ad
prattle and play to it. So God
d youth and puberty and manh
ss with its own piquancy and cha
made it enviable and gracious and
s not to be put by, if it will stand
. Do not think the youth has no fo
se he cannot speak to you and
! in the next   ho spoke
and emphatic   eaven!
t is that very   fulness
m which for   ne noth
at when you   t now
hese words li   es. It se
ows how to   contemp
Bashful   will k
to make   necess
e nonc   are
dinner   muc
d to d   iliate

Ivania Cordero and the words of Ralph Waldo Emerson's "Self-Reliance."

Self-Renewal *by Louise Erdrich*

In early spring I sit down on the old grass of winter and breathe the newness rising from the earth. In the roots, life is gathering in shy waves of power. After a while, if I breathe deep and slowly, drinking the watery, musical air, I feel a union with something larger, fuller, whole. Just for that moment, I move in harmony with one complex and dedicated design. I suppose that is spirit—the larger configuration—but so is each tough blade of grass my footsteps crush.

I am a grounded creature, and I must answer mail, return phone calls, and deal with the daily trivia of life. Each spring, though, the grass reminds me that if it is true that spirit, flesh, and nature are one

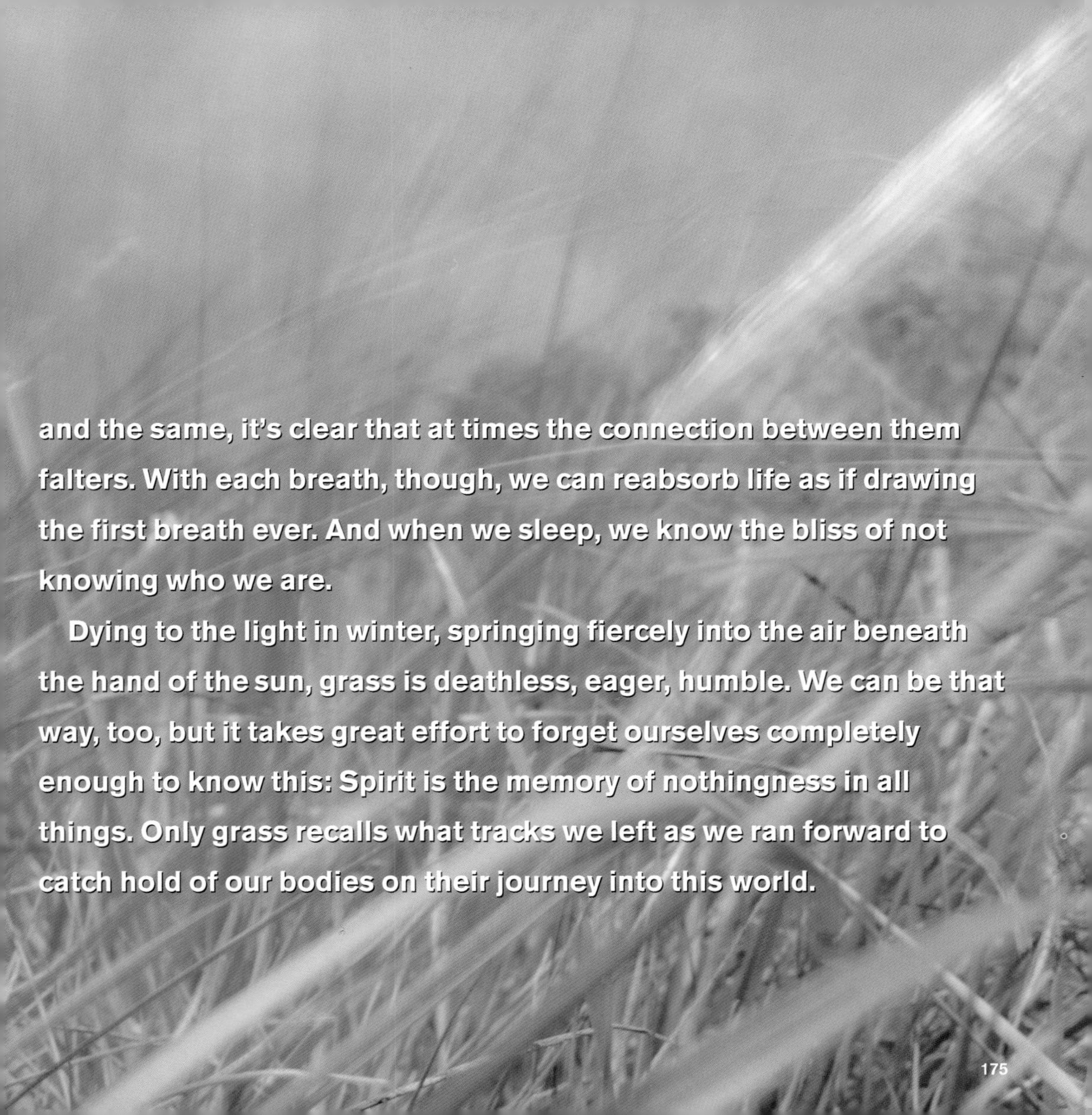

and the same, it's clear that at times the connection between them falters. With each breath, though, we can reabsorb life as if drawing the first breath ever. And when we sleep, we know the bliss of not knowing who we are.

Dying to the light in winter, springing fiercely into the air beneath the hand of the sun, grass is deathless, eager, humble. We can be that way, too, but it takes great effort to forget ourselves completely enough to know this: Spirit is the memory of nothingness in all things. Only grass recalls what tracks we left as we ran forward to catch hold of our bodies on their journey into this world.

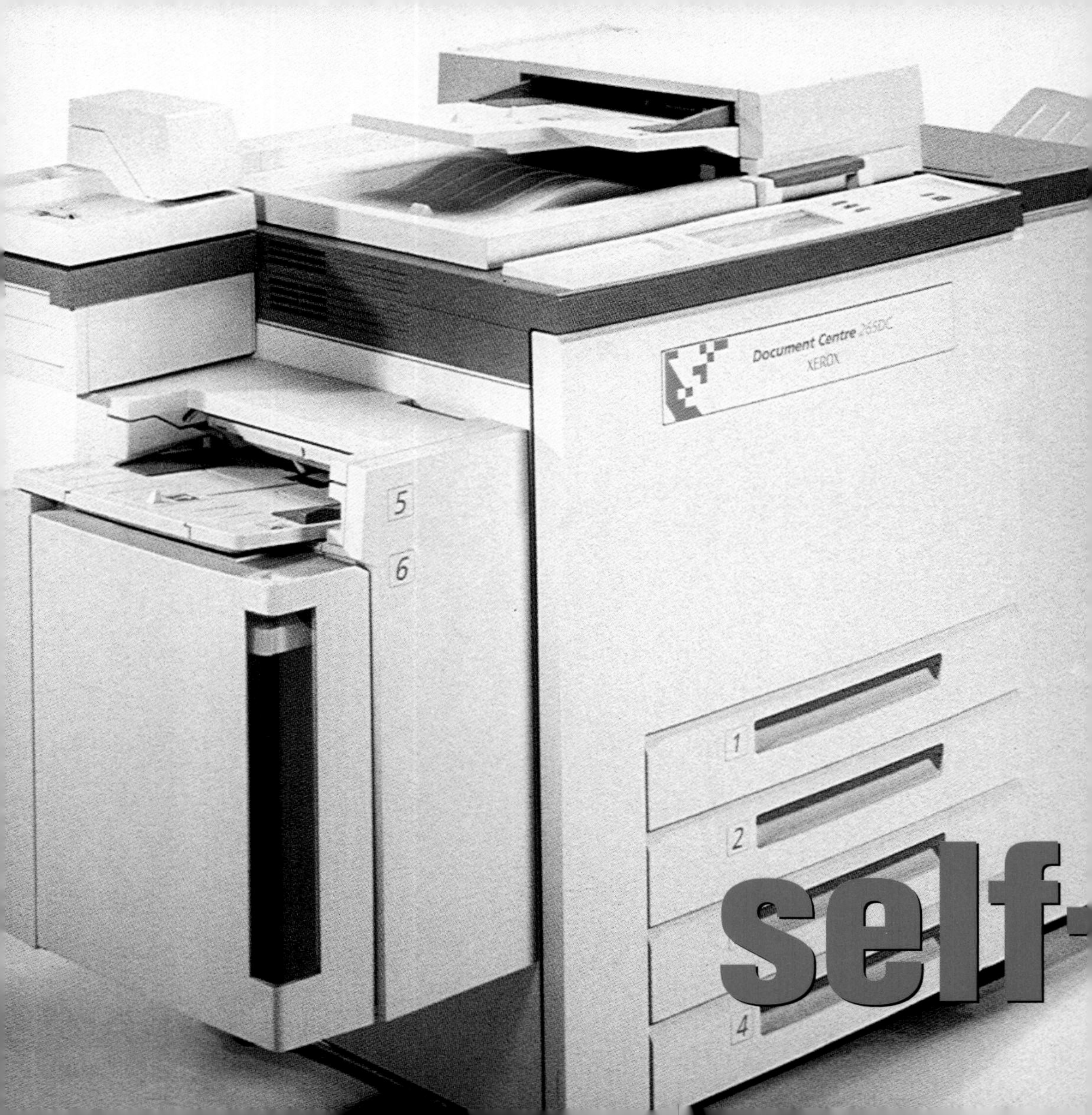
Document Centre 265DC
XEROX
5
6
1
2
4

self-

replicating

"Character—the
to accept
for one's own
the source
self-respect

willingness
responsibility
life–is
from which
springs."
—Joan Didion

SELF-RESPECT

"*This*
To thine
self

above all:

own

be true…"

—WILLIAM SHAKESPEARE

SELF-SC

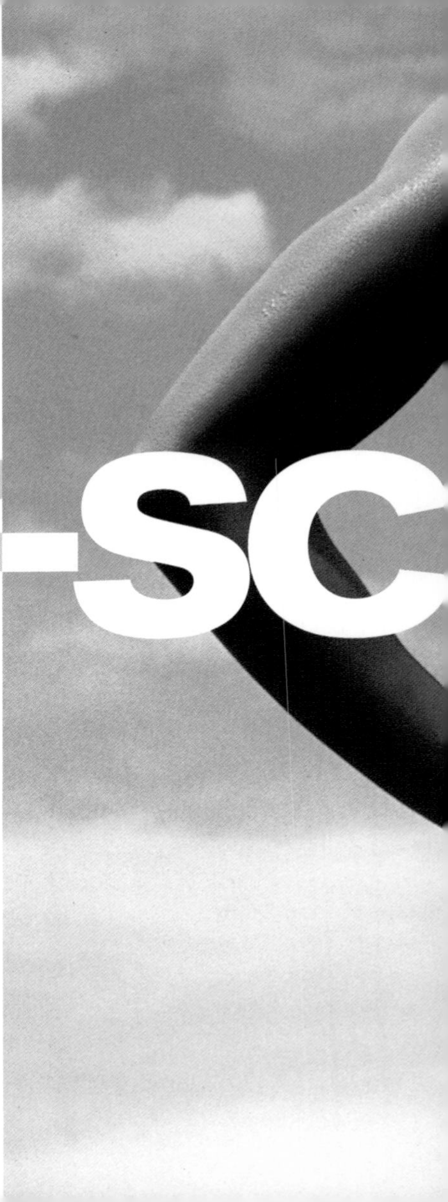

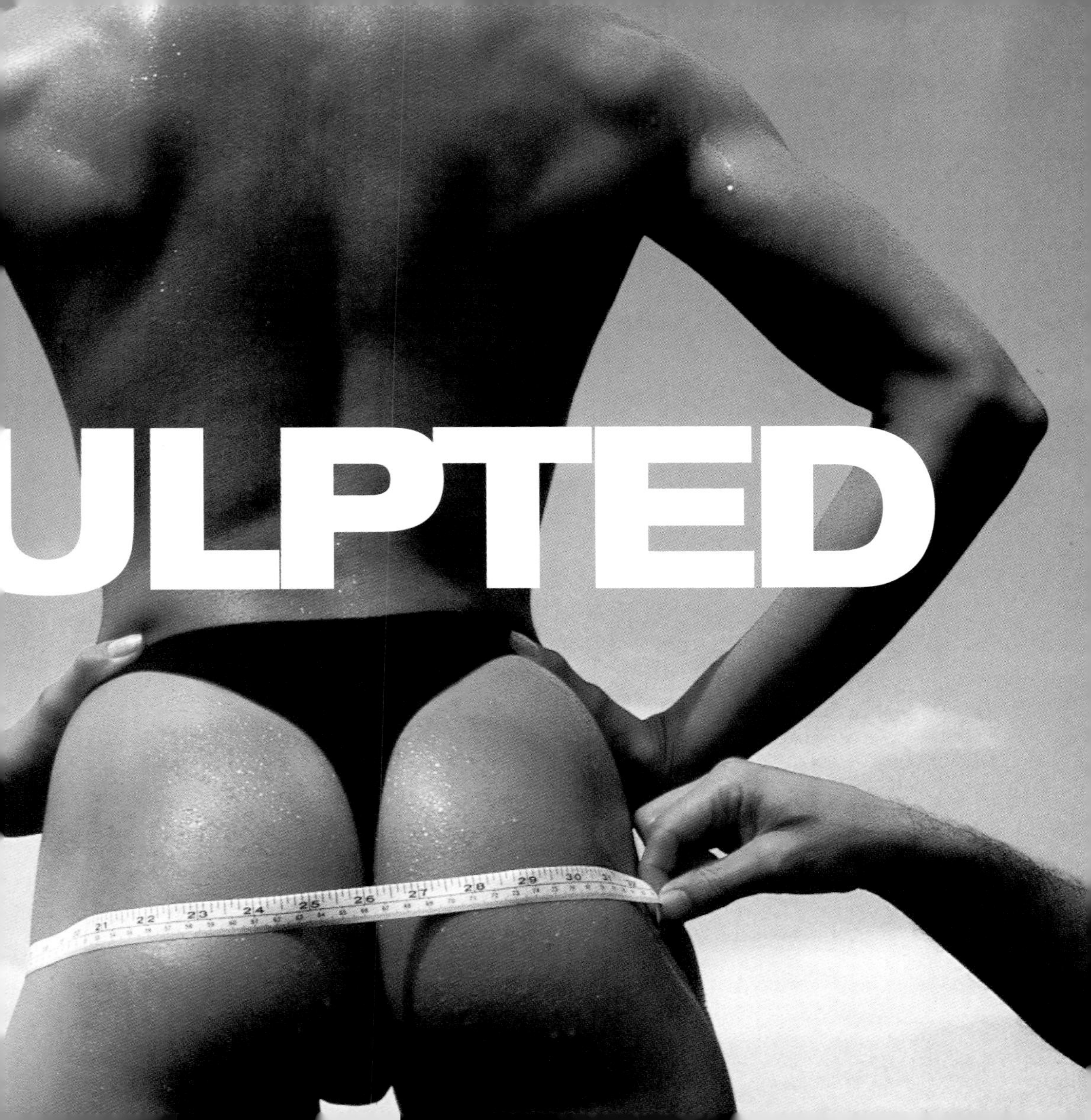
ULPTED

Self-Service

"No man can

try to

without helping

sincerely
help another
himself."
—Ralph Waldo Emerson

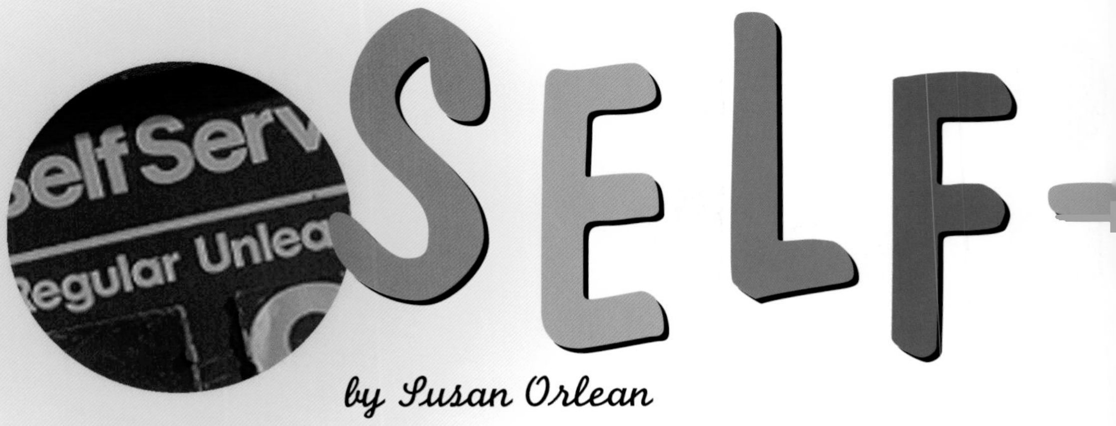
elfServ
Regular Unlea

SELF-

by Susan Orlean

When I was a kid, I had a mysteriously persistent desire to have a job. Girls my age who wanted to work had one choice, professionally speaking, which was babysitting. After a few tries, I realized I was an inept and somewhat indifferent babysitter. My heart was already set on another vocation, anyhow: I desperately wanted to pump gas.

This was a million and a half years ago, before self-serve gas became the standard; this was a moment in history when getting gas meant that the gas-station guy came to the driver's side of the car and asked what he could get for you, and while he filled the tank, he squeegeed the windows and sometimes even poked around under the hood. When the gas pump gave that final click, he'd yank it out and then take your money or credit card and disappear into the office for a moment or two while the tangy aroma of gasoline settled all around. Why did I want to pump gas? I suppose I thought the big hoses and nozzles were cool, and I did love squeegeeing, although at my adolescent height of 4'10", I barely reached the windshield. I craved the smell of gas, and I liked cars, even though I knew nothing about how they worked or how to drive

SERVE

them. Mostly, though, I think I loved the crisp, efficient routine of it, the mechanical purity of the process, or something like that. Pumping gas seemed sort of powerful and cool and tough, and it also seemed really important—something vital to your existence—while everything else in my life (homework, chores, piano lessons) seemed trivial. After all, everybody needed gas and everybody had to rely on the gas-station attendant for it, since there was no such thing as self-serve back then.

My parents were wildly unenthusiastic about my gasoline dreams and they vetoed them, on the grounds that being a gas-station attendant was hot and toxic and noisy; it didn't pay well; it had no future. As luck would have it, I came down with mononucleosis and spent the summer in bed rather than at the pump. By the next summer, I was less interested in gas and more interested in hanging out with my friends. I sort of forgot about the whole episode until a few years ago, when all gas stations became self-serve and I could pump to my heart's content. Whenever I go visit my parents now, I take their cars to the gas station and fill them up, because I can.

SELF-SERVICE

by Suze Orman

I've never been on a plane when the oxygen masks drop, but it's something I've thought about often. Every time we fly we're told that, should the masks drop, if we're traveling with young children, we must first put the oxygen masks on ourselves, and only then lower them over the noses and mouths of our babies. To me, these instructions are nothing short of profound, for they violate what most women feel to be the central truth in their lives: that we must ensure the safety of our loved ones first and foremost, even before we take care of ourselves. I sometimes invoke these airplane instructions when I talk to women about their money, because the instinctive reflex of most women is to put themselves last financially, or at least to put everyone else ahead of themselves. But how can you breathe life-sustaining financial oxygen into the lives of those you love unless you're taking deep strong breaths on your own?

We have come so far in so many ways over the past 20 years—in, for example, what we've all learned about health, exercise, diet. We have made ourselves heard in the workplace, restructured our expectations in our relationships, and given emphasis to the important concept of self-esteem and how to achieve it. If you think of a woman's life as a prism, all these refracted sides to our lives are important, indeed vital. Yet money is also important—indeed vital—to our sustenance, and I do not yet believe that most of us are in a place where we serve ourselves well financially.

If you have not yet plunged into whatever retirement vehicles are available to you, you are not yet breathing well financially, for the time to really assure your financial future is today. If you're in credit card debt, you're not serving yourself well financially. You're also doing yourself a disservice if you allow someone else to have full control of the finances, shower your children with gifts you cannot afford, or do not balance today's needs with those of tomorrow. You must instead know everything there is to know about your money. And you must do everything you can to maximize it.

It doesn't take much money to achieve a state of financial grace; the issue instead is knowing that you are in control of your money, that it passes through you, just the way an airplane's oxygen would, giving you the power and strength to pass on to others. With money, as with an airplane's oxygen, you must serve yourself well, and serve yourself first. Only then will you have the strength, the financial strength, to radiate to those around you.

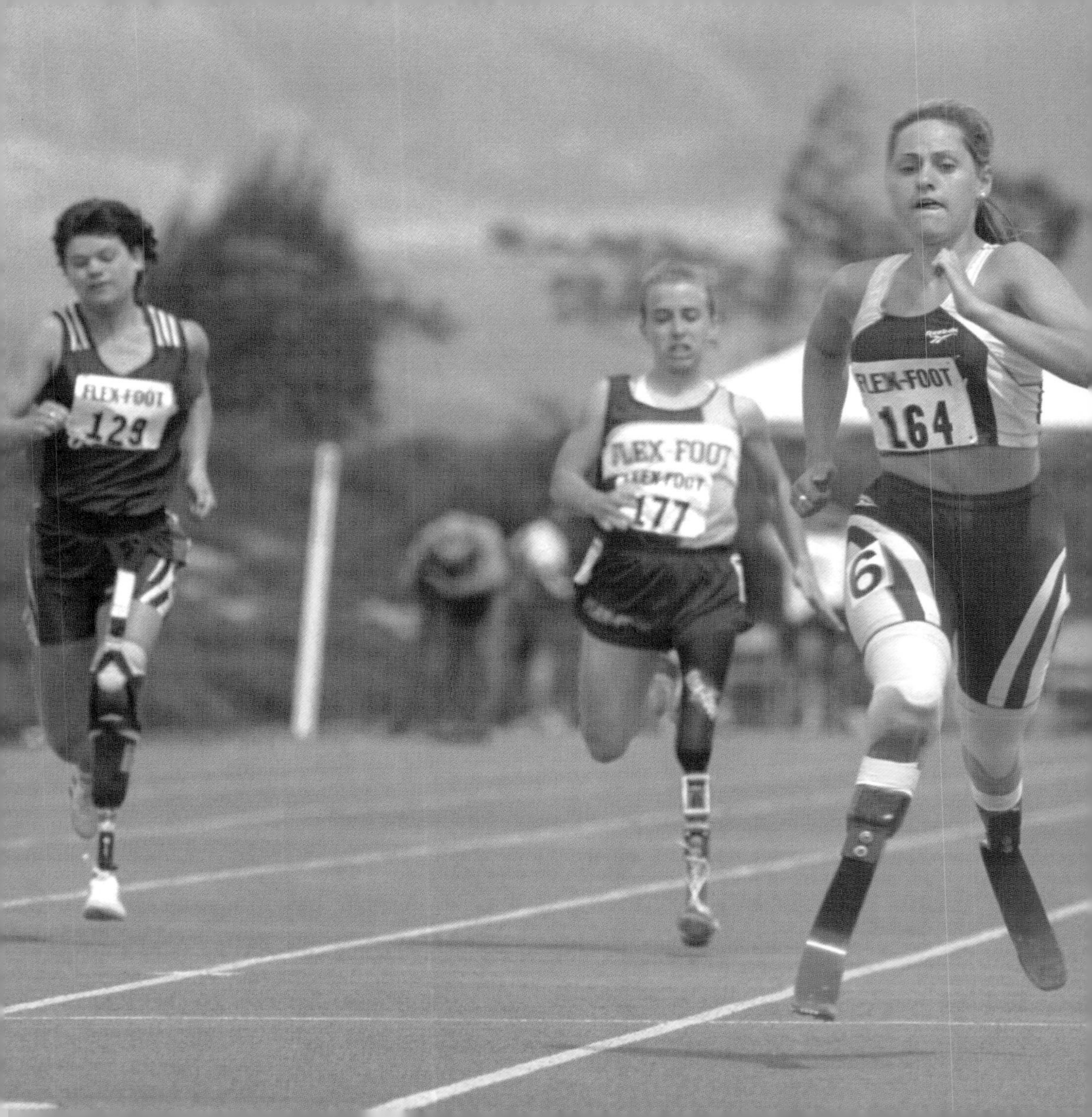
FLEX-FOOT
129
FLEX-FOOT
177
FLEX-FOOT
164

Self-Starter

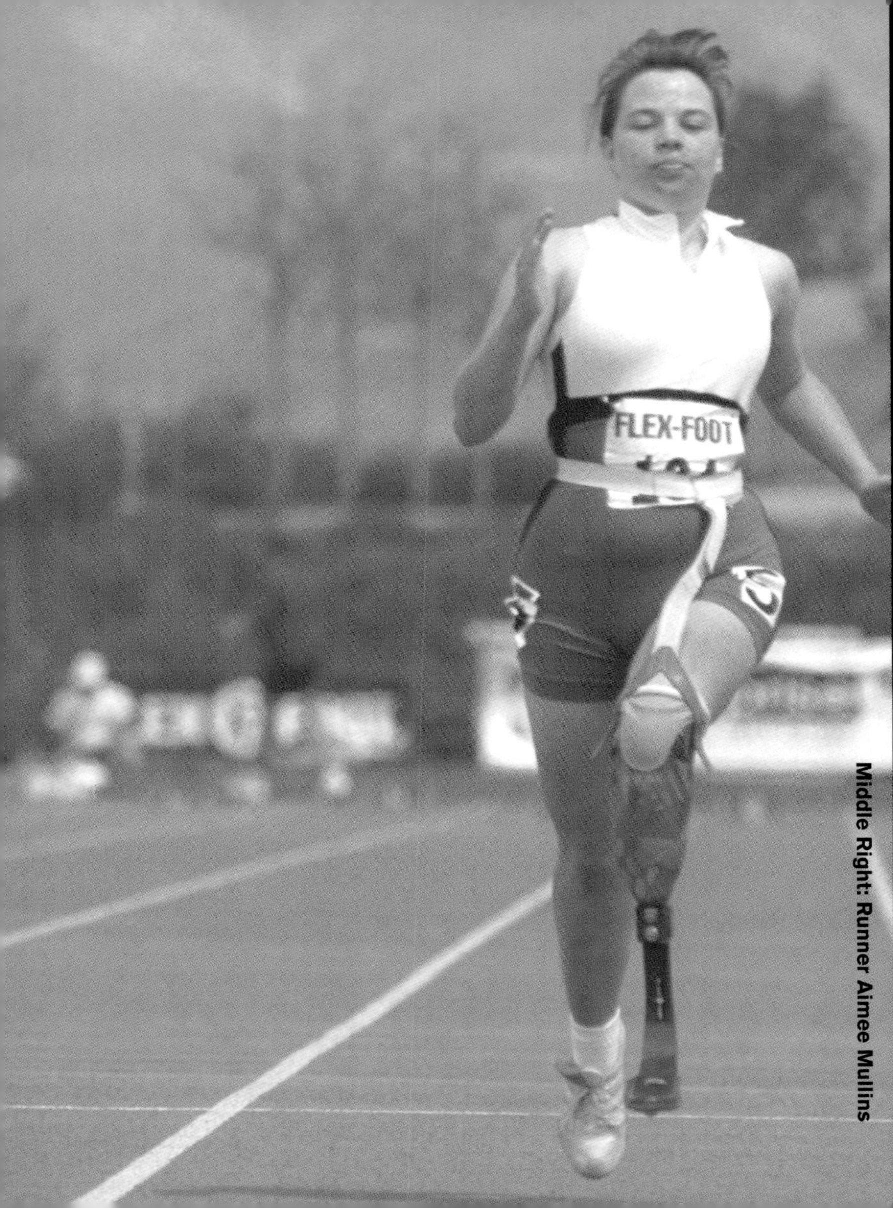
FLEX-FOOT

Middle Right: Runner Aimee Mullins

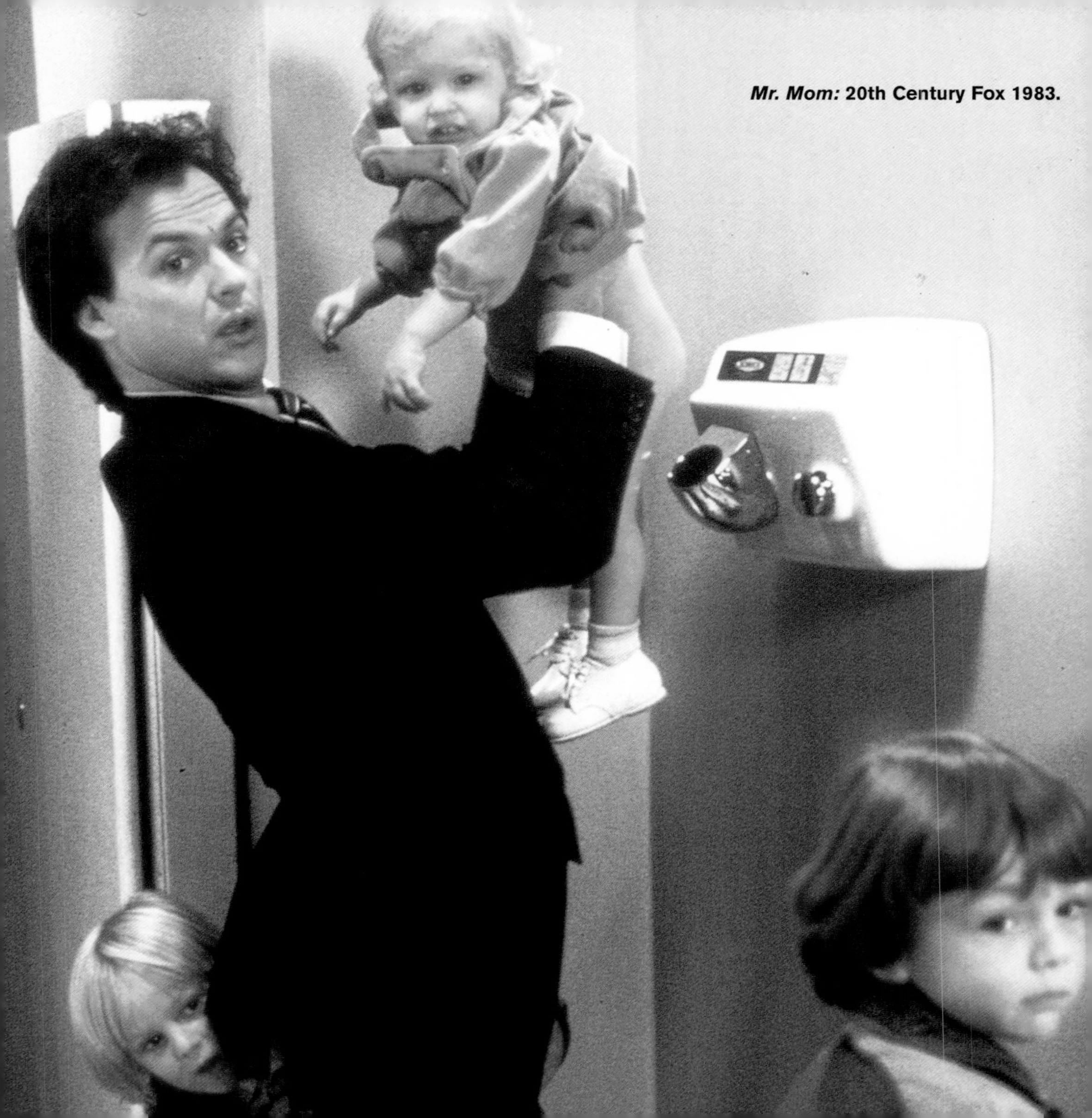

Mr. Mom: **20th Century Fox 1983.**

Self-Sufficient

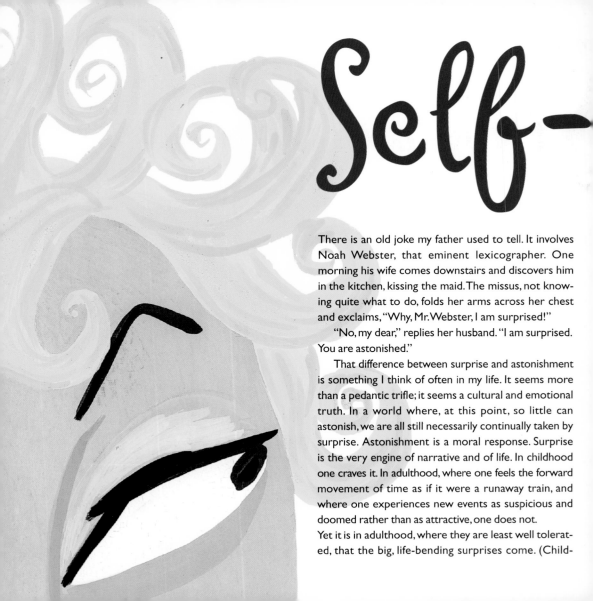

Self-

There is an old joke my father used to tell. It involves Noah Webster, that eminent lexicographer. One morning his wife comes downstairs and discovers him in the kitchen, kissing the maid. The missus, not knowing quite what to do, folds her arms across her chest and exclaims, "Why, Mr. Webster, I am surprised!"

"No, my dear," replies her husband. "I am surprised. You are astonished."

That difference between surprise and astonishment is something I think of often in my life. It seems more than a pedantic trifle; it seems a cultural and emotional truth. In a world where, at this point, so little can astonish, we are all still necessarily continually taken by surprise. Astonishment is a moral response. Surprise is the very engine of narrative and of life. In childhood one craves it. In adulthood, where one feels the forward movement of time as if it were a runaway train, and where one experiences new events as suspicious and doomed rather than as attractive, one does not.

Yet it is in adulthood, where they are least well tolerated, that the big, life-bending surprises come. (Child-

Surprise

by Lorrie Moore

hood, where everything is new, is made up of small, daily surprises, quickly absorbed and made familiar.) In my own life, my address, my spouse, my child all took me by surprise. A New Yorker, I am still stunned that I live in Wisconsin, a state I had associated fondly with Caddie Woodlawn and cheese, but never with myself. Yet the flukes of professional life have landed me here, teaching at the state university. I now drink the local water, speak the local speak, read the local rag, pay the local taxes. I prune the viburnum and fret about the governor.

As for my Wisconsinite husband, I met him on a blind date that was never intended to get that out of hand. We were introduced by friends as provisional amusement for each other, something to do for the semester. Surprise! Now we have rings and vows and anniversaries.

Our little boy was adopted at a week's notice and without any of the standard efforts; we had been thinking of other things, standing still, minding our own business. We were sitting ducks, cigar-store Indians, selfish yuppies. A phone call from a lawyer, a visit to a birth mother, a long lunch in a hamburger joint where we all brooded excitedly over french fries: Now we have a baby we could not live without. And as with all loved babies, he has wrecked our lives and laid siege to our hearts. There we were, in the kitchen, blithely kissing the maid, when Cupid, the Stork, Random Fate, and Santa Claus all walked in and caught us.

Thank God, of course, that surprise is also the very soul of humor. It lends a balance to one's existence. When at the end of our days the Grim Reaper makes his entrance, no doubt we will be less outraged than strangely, comically, caught off guard. "Why me; why now?" is the cry not only of the dying, but of the marrying, the laboring, and the guy slipping on the banana peel. The essential ingredients of heartbreak and accident are the same ones for slapstick: love and wit. They are lying all around us like rich, rich dirt. At least that is the case here in Wisconsin, where, after all, it is farm country. And where I am shocked—shocked!—that I live.

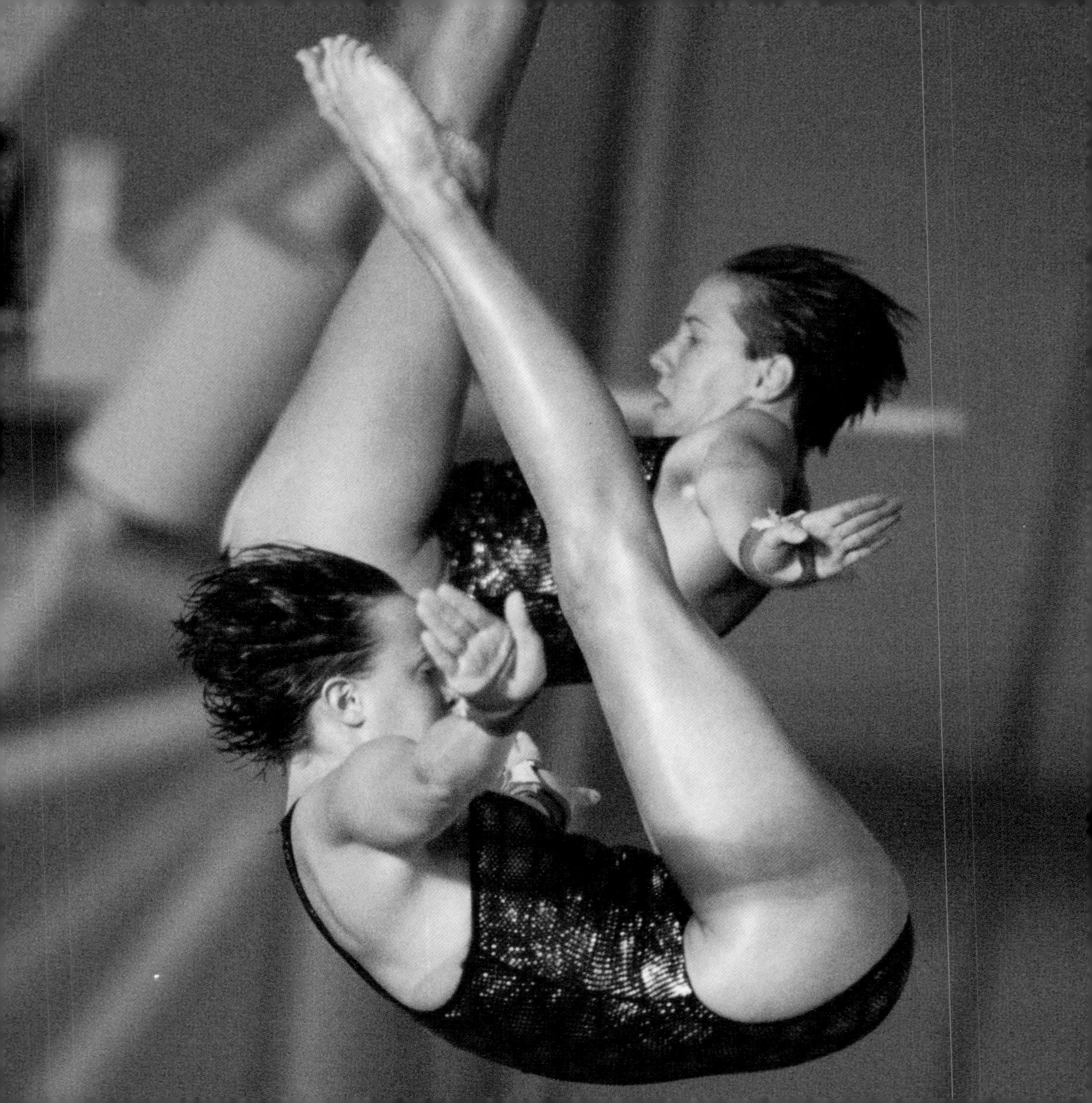

SELF-TIMING

Selflessness

by Cynthia Ozick

Selflessness and self-sacrifice are not the same. Self-sacrifice is the product of pliancy, timidity, cowardice. It is the delusional nobility of the weak. Selflessness, in contrast, emerges from strength—from confidence and courage. Inaction can be a form of selflessness. On a small scale, it means the grit to abstain from asking self-promoting favors. On a larger scale, it points to a determination to relieve a friend of the imposition of an insupportable burden.

It is the more celebrated selflessness of action that we chiefly admire—the indefatigable doers, unsung carriers of bedpans, doctors and nurses who at their own peril minister to AIDS patients, Peace Corps activists who submit to unaccustomed and grueling hardship, serious volunteers in slums and ghettos, social workers, empathic men and women dedicated to public and private charities, and all the rest who grieve for an unredeemed world, who are mindful of the widow and the orphan and the starving and the unloved. Yet no one can do good in the absence of strength and self-reliance and confidence and courage. Good works do not grow out of weakness.

Most of us are not truly self-reliant in the Emersonian sense. Emerson asks us to put our own necessities first, by putting off those who would get in our way. We know we don't have that right; we have no genius; we don't require hands-off cosseting for the sake of our superiority. Nor are many of us so self-sacrificing that we would abase ourselves before the demands of another person's self-regard while abandoning all our hopes and yearnings. And finally, who among us is actually selfless in a daily way? Among the young women I am acquainted with—and fiercely esteem—I count a social worker and a chaplain for the terminally ill. Their compassionate devotion is remarkable. But I am neither social worker nor chaplain, and probably you aren't, either. My own selflessness is that of inaction, and on the smallest scale of all: I can earnestly promise that I will try not to ask you for a favor.

Contributors

9 THE TALMUD
The Talmud is the authoritative body of oral Jewish tradition.

10 INTRODUCTION: THE MEANING OF SELF
Shirley Abbott is a memoirist whose latest book, *Love's Apprentice*, was recently released in paperback. She is also the author of *The Bookmaker's Daughter* and *Womenfolk*.

12 SELF-COLLAGE
Mark Finkenstaedt has worked for *The Washington Post* and *The Los Angeles Times*. Geoffrey Croft has been a Condé Nast Publications contributor for 14 years.

14 SELF-ABSORBED
Photographer Stephanie Rausser's work has appeared in such magazines as *US*, *Glamour*, and SELF. She has also done ad work for Levi's, IBM, Lycra, and Joe Boxer.

16 SELF-ADMITTED
Jeff Stephens is originally from West Texas. His clients include Neiman Marcus, Nordstrom, Cole-Haan, and Crabtree & Evelyn, among others.

18 SELF-ADVERTISEMENT
Stephanie Dolgoff is the executive editor of *Glamour* magazine.

20 SELF-AGGRANDIZEMENT
Chuck Shotwell, a native of Chicago, has been an award-winning photographer for the past 25 years. Both his commercial and art photography are known internationally.

22 SELF-AMUSED
Howard Schatz lives and works in New York City with his wife and business partner, Beverly Ornstein. His photographs are shown in museums and photography galleries internationally and have been published in numerous periodicals as well as in nine books of photography.

24 SELF-ASSURANCE
Ruth Whitney recently retired after 31 years as Editor-in-Chief of *Glamour* magazine.

26 SELF-CENTERED
Photographer Sam Walsh has worked with several adventure and sports magazines, such as *Outside*, *Men's Journal*, *Ski*, *Skiing*, and *Travel & Leisure Golf*.

28 SELF-CLEANING
Davies + Starr have published their work in SELF, *Details*, *Allure*, and *Esquire*.

30 SELF-CONFIDENCE
Janis Joplin (1943–1970) was one of the country's most popular rock and blues singers and is considered by many to be the icon of sixties counterculture.

32 SELF-CONFIDENCE
Liza Nelson's first novel, *Playing Botticelli*, will be published in winter 1999–2000 by Putnam.

34 SELF-CONFIDENCE
Camryn Manheim is the Emmy-award-winning actress who plays defense attorney Ellenor Frutt on the celebrated ABC drama, *The Practice*. This photo was taken by Paul Jasmin and appeared in the May 1999 issue of SELF magazine.

36 SELF-CONFIDENCE
Ron Lynch's photo-
graphs have appeared
in *Glamour*, SELF, and
Harper's Bazaar. He
has also worked for such
companies as J.Crew and
Gap. This photograph
first appeared in SELF
magazine in December
1982.

38 SELF-
CONSCIOUSNESS
Alain de Botton is a
29-year-old British
novelist, author of *On
Love* and *How Proust
Can Change Your Life*.

40 SELF-CONTAINED
Kate Spade is a handbag
designer in New York
City. Here she is pho-
tographed by Patrick
McCarthy, a regular con-
tributor to SELF. Styled
by Eve Feuer. Makeup by
Rebecca for Garren, NYC.
Hair by Marco Scott for
Susan Price, Inc.

42 SELF-CONTAINED
Bebe Moore Campbell

is the author of *Your
Blues Ain't Like Mine,
Brothers and Sisters*, and
*Singing in the Comeback
Choir*. This piece origi-
nally appeared in SELF
magazine in June 1994.

44 SELF-CRITICAL
The late Julian Allen—
best known for his
illustrations of Richard
Nixon and Watergate—
was a staff artist at
*The New York Times
Magazine*. His work
also appeared in *Rolling
Stone, Esquire, Details,
Sports Illustrated,
Newsweek*, and
The New Yorker.

46 SELF-DECEPTION
Lisa Schermerhorn
has done work for
Entertainment Weekly
and *Papyrus*.

48 SELF-DEFENSE
Linda Fairstein has
supervised the sex crimes
prosecution unit of the
New York county district
attorney's office for two

decades. She is also the
author of *Sexual Violence:
Our War Against Rape*
and three crime novels,
*Final Jeopardy, Likely to
Die*, and *Cold Hit*, which
have all become interna-
tional bestsellers.

50 SELF-DEFINITION
Karen Elizabeth
Gordon's wanderlust
fiction includes *Paris
Out of Hand* and *The Red
Shoes and Other Tattered
Tales*. She is also the
creator of strange, goth-
ic, spellbinding language
handbooks such as
*The Deluxe Transitive
Vampire, The Disheveled
Dictionary*, and *Out of the
Loud Hound of Darkness*.

52 SELF-DELUDED
Illinois-born Tom
Sullivan (1963–1994)
went to the Chicago
Art Institute with
his future wife, the
designer Cynthia
Rowley. Sullivan
was an old-fashioned
romantic who took

every opportunity to photograph people kissing.

54 SELF-DENIAL
Art: Photograph by
Davies + Starr.
Text: Richard Klein is
the author of *Cigarettes
Are Sublime* and *Eat Fat*.
He is finishing a book on
jewelry.

56 SELF-
DEPRECATION
Susan Isaacs' most
recent books are the
novel *Red, White and
Blue* and *Brave Dames
and Wimpettes: What
Women Are Really Doing
on Page and Screen*.

58 SELF-
DETERMINATION
Laura Evans, founder of
the Expedition Inspiration
Fund for Breast Cancer
Research and author of
The Climb of My Life,
has dedicated her life
to raising awareness
and funds to help find
a cure for breast cancer.
She originally published

this piece in SELF magazine in January 1995.

60 SELF-DIRECTED
Eliza Gran's work has appeared in *The New York Times, Glamour, Elle, Shape, Travel & Leisure, Town & Country,* and *The Los Angeles Times Magazine.* Her work has also appeared at the L.A. gallery Storyapolis.

62 SELF-DISCOVERY
Louisa Ermelino is the author of the novel *Joey Dee Gets Wise.*

64 SELF-DISCOVERY
Penny Gentieu has done 150 covers for magazines such as *Time, Newsweek,* SELF, and *Parenting.* Her book *Wow! Babies!* published in 1997, was named Best Children's Book by *Parents* magazine. Her most recent book is *Baby! Talk!*

66 SELF-DISCOVERY
Gabrielle "Coco" Chanel

(1883–1971) revolutionized women's fashion in the 1920s.

68 SELF-DOUBT
Anna Palma is from Iceland. She works mainly for magazines, including *Parenting, Vogue Bambini, Newsweek, Mademoiselle,* and SELF, photographing children, fashion, and beauty.

70 SELF-EFFACING
Keith Lathrop has lived and worked in Paris since 1991. His photographs have appeared in *Cosmopolitan, Glamour,* and SELF. This photo appeared in the May 1999 issue of SELF.

72 SELF-EMPLOYED
Lauren Greenfield's work has appeared in many magazines, including *Harper's, Time, Life,* and *The New York Times Magazine,* and in such museums as the Harvard University

Archive, The Museum of Fine Arts in Houston, and The Jewish Museum of New York. Her book, *Fast Forward: Growing Up in the Shadow of Hollywood,* was published in 1997 and is being made into a film by Tristar.

74 SELF-ESTEEM
Mike Twohy's cartoons appear in *The New Yorker* magazine on a regular basis. His work has appeared in a great many other publications, including *The National Law Journal* and *USA Weekend.*

76 SELF-ESTEEM
Cindy Crawford is a model.

78 SELF-ESTEEM
These quotes were gathered from girls who are members of Girls Incorporated, a national nonprofit organization dedicated to inspiring all girls to be strong, smart, and bold.

80 SELF-ESTEEM
Roz Chast's cartoons appear in *The New Yorker* magazine, *The Sciences, Harvard Business Review,* and many other magazines. Ms. Chast has also published several cartoon collections and has illustrated four children's books, most recently *Meet My Staff.*

82 SELF-ESTEEM
Miss Piggy (birth year not revealed) is a star of both television and film. She is best known for her work on *The Muppet Show* and the Muppet movies. She is skilled in karate.

84 SELF-EXPOSURE
See Self-Absorbed.

86 SELF-EXPRESSION
Pulitzer Prize–winning journalist Anna Quindlen is the author of many fiction and nonfiction books, including *One True Thing, Black*

and *Blue*, and *Siblings*.
This piece originally
appeared in SELF
in May 1993.

88 SELF-EXPRESSION
Mae West (1890–1982)
was arguably the first
sex goddess of the silver
screen. Her film credits
include *Sextette* and
Myra Breckenridge.

90 SELF-GENERATED
Didier Gault's work
has appeared in
Modern Bride, SELF,
Marie Claire, *Fitness*,
and *Shape*.

92 SELF-GOVERNING
Timothy Greenfield-
Sanders' work has
appeared in *Vanity
Fair*, *The New York
Times Magazine*, *InStyle*,
and *Index*. Last year
he directed a feature
film called *Lou Reed
Rock and Roll Heart*,
which was nominated
for a Grammy Award.

94 SELF-HEALING
Bernie S. Siegel, M.D., is
the author of the
bestselling books
*Love, Medicine &
Miracles* and *Peace,
Love & Healing*.
His newest book,
Prescriptions for Living,
is about how to heal
your own life. This piece
originally appeared in
SELF in July 1993.

96 SELF-HELP
Peter Steiner has been
a nationally recognized
cartoonist for approxi-
mately 20 years. His
work regularly appears
in *The New Yorker*.
Other cartoons by
Steiner may be seen
in *The Washington Times*
and *The Weekly Standard*.

98 SELF-HELP
Elizabeth Berg is the
author of seven novels,
the latest being *Until
the Real Thing Comes
Along*, as well as a new
book on writing, called
Escaping Into the Open.

100 SELF-HYPNOSIS
See Self-Directed.

102-105 SELF-
IDENTIFIED
Credits appear on pages.

106 SELF-IMAGE
Art: This photograph
is by Robert Fleischauer,
whose work has appeared
in such magazines as
Mademoiselle, *Paper*, and
Surface. Text: Lauren
Hutton is a model and
actress who has been in
the public eye for 30 years.

108 SELF-IMAGE
Mary Ellen Mark's
work has appeared in
such magazines as *Rolling
Stone*, *Vanity Fair*, *US*,
Entertainment Weekly,
Texas Monthly, and SELF.
She has been awarded
several NEA fellowships
and Hasselblad awards.
She has also won a
Guggenheim fellowship.

110 SELF-
IMPOSED EXILE
Art: Photograph by

Chuck Baker. See Self-
Replicating. Text: Annette
O'Toole is an actress,
who has also always been
a writer. She is currently
at work on a novel.

112 SELF-
INDULGENCE
Art: Ariel Skelley was a
contributing photographer
at SELF magazine for
seven years. She has
worked for several
Condé Nast magazines
as well as for Disney,
Proctor and Gamble,
and AT&T. This picture
originally appeared in
SELF in May 1987.
Text: These quotes
appeared in SELF in
May 1990. They were
collected by author
Cree McCree.

114 SELF-INVENTION
Diane Johnson is the
author of *Persian Nights*,
Le Divorce (nominated
for a National Book
Award in 1997), and a
forthcoming novel, also
set in Paris.

116 SELF-INVOLVED
Art: Andrea Blanch's most recent book is *Italian Men, Love and Sex.* Her photographs have been published in many magazines and she has lectured at the Smithsonian Institute on fashion photography. This photo originally appeared in SELF magazine. Text: National Public Radio commentator Marion Winik is the author of *Telling, First Comes Love,* and *The Lunch-Box Chronicles: Notes From the Parenting Underground,* books that stand on the very frontier of literary self-involvement.

118 SELF-JUDGING
See Self-Governing.

120 SELF-KNOWLEDGE
David Ansen is the movie critic for *Newsweek.* He has also written television documentaries on Greta Garbo, Groucho Marx, and Bette Davis. A longer version of this piece originally appeared in SELF magazine in October 1997.

122 SELF-KNOWLEDGE
Lao-Tzu (c. 604 B.C.) is regarded as the originator of Taoist philosophy. His only surviving work, *Tao the King,* has been widely translated.

124 SELF-LOATHING
Alice Hoffman is the author of 12 novels, including *Property Of, Illumination Night, Seventh Heaven, Turtle Moon, Second Nature, Practical Magic* (recently released as a number one motion picture), and *Here On Earth,* which was a selection of Oprah's book club. Her collection of stories, *Local Girls,* was published by Putnam last June.

126 SELF-LOVE
Lucille Ball (1911–1989), a television, film, and Broadway star, was best known for her long-running 1950s sitcom, *I Love Lucy.*

128 SELF-LOVE
Lucy Grealy is the author of a memoir, *Autobiography of a Face,* numerous essays, and a novel from Doubleday coming in winter 1999.

130 SELF-MADE
Connie Porter is the author of the Addy series, six historical children's novels, and also has written two adult novels, *All-Bright Court* (Houghton Mifflin, 1991) and *Imani All Mine* (Houghton Mifflin, 1999).

132 SELF-MASTERY
Controversial photographer Robert Mapplethorpe was a classicist and a formalist. Best known for his erotic work—which created quite a stir with the National Endowment for the Arts—Mapplethorpe himself thought the subject matter unimportant to his artistic vision, which had to do with a sense of universal sexual possibility.

134 SELF-MEDICATING
Art: See Self-Cleaning. Text: Teacher, columnist, and novelist Susan Cheever is the author of nine books, including *Note Found in a Bottle,* a memoir about drinking. She is currently writing a book about raising her two children.

28 SELF-OPERATING
This photograph, *Sunset Over Ocean* was shot by Peter Gridley in 1988.

136 SELF-PERPETUATING
Lauren Slater is the author of *Welcome to*

My Country and *Prozac Diary*. Her book *Learning to Fall* will be published by Random House in February 2000.

138 SELF-PITY
Patricia Marx writes for TV, movies, magazines, and books. She is the co-author of *The Skinny (What Every Skinny Woman Knows About Dieting—And Won't Tell You!)* and *Meet My Staff,* a children's book illustrated by Roz Chast.

140 SELF-PLEASING
Joshua Greene's photos have appeared in many Condé Nast magazines, including SELF, *Glamour, Vogue,* and *House and Garden.* He has done 14 photo books, his latest being *Modern Antiques for the Table,* which was co-authored by Sheila Chefetz.

142 SELF-PORTRAIT
In 1996 a retrospective of Nan Goldin's work

was organized by The Whitney Museum of American Art in New York City. Goldin has received numerous grants and awards, and her photographs have been exhibited worldwide. Her books include: *The Other Side* (1992), *I'll Be Your Mirror* (1996) and *Couples and Loneliness* (1998).

144 SELF-PORTRAIT
Charley Yoshimura is the five-year-old son of *Self-Defined*'s editor, Sara Nelson. Sasha Listfield Dudding is the five-year-old daughter of SELF Magazine's Articles Editor, Emily Listfield.

146 SELF-PORTRAIT
Annie Leibovitz is known for her photographic portraits. She was Chief Photographer at *Rolling Stone* before helping to relaunch *Vanity Fair* in 1981, where she became the magazine's first contributing photographer.

148 SELF-PORTRAIT
Left: The actress Jamie Lee Curtis also writes children's books. Her most recent one is called *Today I Feel Silly & Other Moods That Make My Day*. Right: Molly Shannon is a member of the cast of *Saturday Night Live*.

150 SELF-PORTRAIT
Sofonisba Anguissola (1535–1625) was an Italian painter. This work, *Self-Portrait, Painting the Madonna,* 1556, belongs to the Muzeum Zamek W. Lancucie, Lancut, Poland.

Elizabeth Vigee-LeBrun (1755–1842) was a French artist famous for her portraits of Marie Antoinette. This work hangs in the Uffizi, Florence, Italy.

Mary Cassatt (1844–1926) was an American Impressionist. This

self-portrait is part of the collection of the National Portrait Gallery in Washington, D.C.

Frida Kahlo (1907–1954) was a Mexican artist. Her *Self-Portait with Monkey* belongs to the Museum Robert Brady, Cuernevaca, Mexico.

152 SELF-PORTRAIT
Anne Brigman (1869–1950) was known for allegorical studies, nudes, and draped figures in landscapes.

Lee Miller (1907–1977) was a fashion photographer for *Vogue* in London as well as a war correspondent who recorded the liberation of Paris and the Dachau and Buchenwald concentration camps.

Imogen Cunningham (1883–1976) was a photographer admired for her crisp black-and-white works, and her portraits and nature studies.

154 SELF-POSSESSED
The Australian photographer and commercial director Denis Piel has produced work for *Vogue*, *Elle*, and *The New York Times Magazine*. He directed a documentary, *Love is Blind*, in 1995.

156 SELF-PROMO-TION/SELF PARODY
Anita Kunz's work has appeared in *Time*, *Rolling Stone*, and *The New York Times Magazine*.

158 SELF-PROMOTION
T-shirt and photo courtesy of SELF magazine.

160 SELF-PROPELLED
Norwegian Catherine Wessel has lived in New York City for the past 10 years and has published her pictures in *Italian Glamour*, *Vogue*, *Outside*, *National Geographic Adventurer*, and SELF. She has also done ad work for Nike, Adidas, and Sony.

162 SELF-PROTECTION
Art: See Self-Cleaning. Text: Karin Cook is the author of the novel *What Girls Learn* and the director of public relations for The Door, New York City's oldest and largest multiservice youth center. She was the National Health Educator for Condomania.

164 SELF-QUESTIONING
Adam Olszewski's work has appeared in the magazines *Surface*, *W*, *Jane*, and *Women's Wear Daily*. This picture was published in *D* magazine, an Italian publication.

166 SELF-REFERENTIAL/SELF-REVERENTIAL
Art, left: John Huba is a working photographer based in New York City. He has done both fashion and portraiture for publications such as *Town & Country*, *The New York Times Magazine*, *Vanity Fair*, *Interview*, *Travel & Leisure*, and *W*. Recently he began to direct and is responsible for the Old Navy TV campaign. Art, right: Kevin Westenberg photographs for *US*, *Rolling Stone*, *New Musical Express*, and *Mojo*, among many other magazines.

168 SELF-REFLECTIVE
Jim Jordan's work has been in international editions of *Marie Claire*, *Vogue*, and many other magazines.

170 SELF-REGARD
Danzy Senna is the author of *Caucasia*, a novel. Her writings on race and gender have appeared in SELF, *Glamour*, *Newsweek*, and several anthologies. She lives in Brooklyn and is currently working on her second novel.

172 SELF-RELIANCE
Tim Rollins, an artist and teacher, founded Tim Rollins + K.O.S. (Kids of Survival), a collaborative art organization for at-risk youth. Their works have been displayed in museums and galleries around the country, including the Modern Museum of Art in New York City.

174 SELF-RENEWAL
Louise Erdrich writes both fiction and nonfiction. Her titles include *Love Medicine*, *Tales of Burning Love*, and *The Antelope Wife*. This piece originally appeared in SELF magazine in July 1994.

Photographer Russell Kaye contributes to many magazines including SELF.

176 SELF-REPLICATING
Art, left: Photo courtesy of the Xerox Corporation. Art, right: Chuck Baker has worked for SELF, *The New York Times Magazine*, and *New York* magazine. His book, *Garden Ornament*, was published in June by Clarkson Potter.

178 SELF-RESPECT
Onetime *Vogue* editor Joan Didion has written numerous essays, works of fiction, and screenplays, including *A Book of Common Prayer*, *The White Album*, and *Salvador*.

180 SELF-RESPECT
William Shakespeare (1564–1616), the most famous English playwright and poet, saw his comedies, tragedies, and histories staged at the Globe theater.

182 SELF-SCULPTED
Michel Comte has worked for many Condé Nast magazines, including *Italian Vogue* and *Vogue*. This photo originally appeared in SELF in September 1983.

184 SELF-SERVICE
Ralph Waldo Emerson (1803–1882) was an essayist, poet, and leader of the Transcendental Movement. Emerson's most famous essay, "Self-Reliance," was published in 1841.

186 SELF-SERVE
New Yorker staff writer Susan Orlean is the author of *Saturday Night* and the recently acclaimed *The Orchid Thief*.

188 SELF-SERVICE
Suze Orman is the best-selling author of *The 9 Steps to Financial Freedom* as well as the recently released *The Courage to Be Rich*. She is a columnist for SELF magazine and a frequent guest on *Oprah*.

190 SELF-STARTER
Lynn Johnson has produced photo essays for such notable publications as *National Geographic*, *German Geo*, *Life*, *Stern*, *Time*, *People*, and *Sports Illustrated*, among others. Born without fibula bones in both shins, double amputee Aimee Mullins is a model, an actress, and an athlete. She holds world records in the 100 and 200 meter dashes, and the long jump.

192 SELF-SUFFICIENT
This picture of the actor Michael Keaton is a still from the 1983 20th Century Fox film, *Mr. Mom*.

194 SELF-SURPRISE
Art: Illustration by Carlotta for Kramer & Kramer. Text: Novelist and short story writer Lorrie Moore's latest collection is *Birds of America*.

196 SELF-TIMING
Al Bello's work has appeared in publications such as *Sports Illustrated*, *The New York Times*, *The Los Angeles Times*, and *Maxim* magazine.

29 SELF-WINDING
Photo courtesy of Movado.

198 SELFLESSNESS
Cynthia Ozick is an essayist, novelist and critic whose most recent novel, *The Puttermesser Papers*, was nominated for a National Book Award. "Selflessness" is a shortened version of a piece that originally appeared in SELF magazine in December 1998.

Make Your Own Self-Portrait: Draw It, Photograph It, Write It—Here